HEA Title II-A
D1083262
ORTHOGRAPHIC PROJECTION —
MILES
SCALE CORRECT ONLY ALONG PARALLELS
ARCTIC CIRCLE
Yenisei
Igarka
Norilsk
Ob
Irtysh
Taz
SOUTHERN LIMIT OF PERMAFROST
Mangazeya
Taz Bay
Yamal Pen.
Dikson I.
Vorkhuta
Yugorski Shar
Barents Sea
Archangel
White Sea
Murmansk
Leningrad
EUROPE
30° EAST
SPITS-BERGEN (SVALBARD)
LAPLAND
Kiruna
Sea
MERIDIAN OF GREENWICH 0°
80° NORTH
Oslo
Copenhagen
70°
30° WEST
GREENLAND
King Oscars Fjord
Mesters Vig
60°
ICELAND SEE INSET
50°
40°
30°
Holsteinsborg
BW8
Søndrestrøm Fjord
Davis Strait
Ivigtut
Cape Farewell
Atlantic Ocean
Hamilton Inlet
Goose Bay
Gander
NEWFOUNDLAND
ICELAND
Grimsey
Eyjafjordur
Hallormstadir
Akureyri
Vatnajökull
Denmark Strait
Langjökull
Mt. Hekla
Reykjavik
Keflavik
MILES
0
100
200

HERE IS THE

FAR NORTH

HERE IS THE

FAR NORTH

by Evelyn Stefansson

ILLUSTRATED WITH PHOTOGRAPHS
BY THE AUTHOR AND OTHERS

MAP BY *Richard Edes Harrison*

CHARLES SCRIBNER'S SONS NEW YORK

PRINTED IN THE UNITED STATES OF AMERICA D-1.65[MH]

LIBRARY OF CONGRESS CATALOG CARD NUMBER 57-5667

Contents

FOR *Stef*

AUTHOR'S NOTE

I am deeply indebted to the Government of Iceland which made possible a trip to and through that beautiful and storied land in 1949, and to the Government of Denmark for a memorable journey along the Greenland coast in 1953. Scandinavian Airlines, pioneers in transarctic civilian aviation, made possible my 1955 flight from Los Angeles to Copenhagen by way of arctic Greenland. To the innumerable people who made all these trips fruitful, and whose generous hospitality I can never hope to repay, go my warmest thanks.

This book covers the Far North generally, and Iceland, Greenland and the Soviet Arctic particularly. A previous book, *Here Is Alaska,* soon to appear in a revised edition, describes the United States portion of the Arctic. A book, still to come, will complete the description of the Arctic Circle, with emphasis on the peoples of the Canadian Arctic.

EVELYN STEFANSSON
November 29, 1956

I

Introduction:

THE GREAT CIRCLE FLIGHT

The "Viking," on which the author made her great circle flight.

ONE

The Short Way Is North

THE time was midnight, the place Los Angeles International Airport. A huge plane took off effortlessly. As it soared, the blue lights marking the runways sparkled in the night like long sapphire necklaces. The "Viking" airship gained altitude and the rainbow-hued constellation of the city below grew swiftly in all directions, like a movie scene starting with a close-up that reveals a huge landscape as the camera gradually moves backward. Los Angeles now filled our entire horizon, sparkling, shining and winking.

When at last the glittering city was visible no longer, and the engine noise had been transformed into a hum, comfortable and monotonous, a quiet cultured voice with a barely detectable Scandinavian accent welcomed us aboard the plane, first in English, then in Danish. Flight 932 following a great circle course from Los Angeles to Copenhagen would take twenty-four hours of elapsed time although we should be aboard for two nights and a day. Eight hours would be lost as we passed through various time zones. There would be two refueling stops en route, the first at Winnipeg, the other at Sondrestrom Fjord in Greenland, north of the Arctic Circle. In polite, unemotional tones we were informed that our average cruising speed would be 300 miles an hour, our altitude 17,000 feet. The weather report was good. We might now unfasten our seat belts and a midnight supper would be served.

Excitement percolated through my bones. I was tempted to talk back to the invisible Captain's voice. I wanted to ask why he didn't underline the historic importance of these, the first regularly scheduled civilian overseas passenger flights to land and take off north of the Arctic Circle? Why didn't he explain the strategic reasons for flying to Europe by way of Hudson Bay, Baffin Island, Davis Strait, Greenland and Iceland? This was to be a true great circle course. By flying the shortest route, northeast, east and southeast, instead of straight east, we would save a thousand flight miles. We would save fuel and time too. Why didn't he highlight some of the advantages of arctic over temperate zone flights; point out that the weather would average better; that it would be safer, for unlike most trans-Atlantic flights, we should be flying mainly over land and would never be more than a few hundred miles from an emergency landing field.

Suppressing my desire to rise and address the businessmen, tourists, television producers and journalists who made up the passenger list in the crowded plane, I settled for making an imaginary speech. In moving and eloquent tones I pointed out, silently, of course, that we were to fly over lands discovered and explored by a now extinct breed of hero. Strong, brave and gallant gentlemen like Henry Hudson, Martin Frobisher, William Baffin and John Davis, not forgetting the earliest of all, Erik the Red and his son Leif the Lucky. Though none had succeeded in changing the face of the rugged and austere lands they discovered, all had graciously left behind the gift of place names. Musical Elizabethan names like Hold With Hope, Sir Thomas Roe His Welcome, Lok's Land and Cape Mercy. Erik, who discovered, explored and named Greenland, has been called the first realtor in history. He thought if he gave the new land an attractive name it would be easier to gather colonists, and he proved to be right. Every place name hides a fragment of his-

Tourists to the Arctic may now see sights formerly limited to explorers.

tory—the story of a generous patron, or a beloved friend, or perhaps a comrade newly dead. Sometimes it is a mirror reflecting feelings, whether of exaltation or despair, felt by the men who first looked at these new shores.

For me this flight represented a kind of miracle. A miracle symbolizing the rare moment when theory is transformed into fact; when forecast becomes truth. Let me explain:

Many years ago my arctic explorer husband, Vilhjalmur Stefansson, who discovered new lands and peoples during his many years of arctic work, announced that he foresaw a new and important future for all northern lands. He said the invention of the airplane would change the travel maps of the world and especially the face of the Arctic. The drift ice in the Polar Sea which formed an impenetrable barrier to the stoutest ships since Elizabethan times, and earlier, offers no resistance at all to aircraft. Quite the contrary. With weather slightly less stormy than in temperate zones, with innumerable ready-made emergency landing fields provided free by the floating sea ice, a shorter, great circle course would at last be possible. He argued that every arctic island, wherever it was situated, had a new importance as a potential air base, weather or radio station. Whether large or small it should not be disdained whatever its climate or distance from world centers. The new air routes across the Polar Sea would bring world centers closer to one another. As usual when new ideas are too far ahead of their time and audience, these were considered queer, laughed at or ignored.

Clutched in my hand was a copy of Stef's *The Northward Course of Empire.* In the back of the book was a map drawn long before any arctic flights of consequence had been made, showing potential aviation routes crisscrossing the Arctic. One of the tracks shown might have been drawn especially to illustrate the very flight we were making—thirty-three years later! If Stef was above such matters, I at least was going to enjoy gloating; for it is not often that a prophecy comes true in a prophet's lifetime.

Darkness would be our companion on this flight until just before we arrived in Winnipeg. But from there on, thanks to our northward course and the month of May, we would have daylight until we were well past the middle of the Greenland Ice Cap. Unfolding my polar projection map I drew a line to mark our path. We would enter Hudson Bay's western shore along its lower third, and continuing in a northeasterly direction cross it and approach southern Baffin Island. We would bisect the latter north of Frobisher Bay, skirting the entrance of Cumberland Sound. Next Davis Strait would appear and soon thereafter the fabulous coast of Greenland, the "largest island or smallest continent in the world." Many world travelers who have seen arctic, tropic and temperate lands, for instance the Lindberghs, have said that the approach to the Greenland coast on a sunny day is one of the most startling, breath-taking and beautiful sights on earth.

Sondrestrom Fjord is the longest and most spectacular inlet on the west coast of Greenland and at its head lies BW8. Here we would land. BW8 is short for Bluie West 8, a code name invented during World War II when this was one of the numerous, at first secret, air bases the United States built in the Canadian Arctic and Greenland.

Taking off from BW8 we would cross the largest glacier in the northern hemisphere, second largest in the world, the Greenland Ice Cap. Would the ghosts of Nansen, Peary and the others who had made the traverse afoot come out to greet us? Our course would be eastward crossing the Inland Ice, and then southeastward, as we headed toward Copenhagen over Denmark Straits, then over Iceland, to arrive the next morning in Denmark's capital.

As our plane journey began, the friendly and sometimes excited remarks of fellow passengers reminded me how little the average person knows about the Arctic. And how much of the little he "knows" is often partially or wholly untrue! There is much in the polar regions that is strange to temperate zone dwellers, more that is entirely new, and so much of what is new is complicated and difficult to understand. The situation becomes even more tangled when eager newcomers inquire about a specific part of the Arctic and then apply the answer they receive to the whole North.

But the Arctic is huge—its lands and seas total more than seven *million* square miles, twice as much as the entire United States. Northern Siberia is very different from Spitsbergen, the island group north of Scandinavia. Greenland is on the whole very unlike Alaska. Within Alaska the northern slope differs from the interior, and within the interior the mountainous Brooks Range area is different from the Yukon Flats. It is dangerous to *generalize* about the Arctic! Various parts of it contain differing climates, terrains, animals, vegetation, colors, peoples and cultures.

But don't be intimidated. If many things are different in each section of the Arctic, *some* things are the same. For instance the hours of daylight and darkness, while different from southerly latitudes, operate throughout the Arctic in an orderly, predictable fashion. Everywhere in the Arctic when the weather is fine there is a great clarity of atmosphere such as is not found elsewhere—at least, not north of the equator. The difficulties

Yakutsk
Lena
Oimekon
(Cold Pole of the World)
SIBERIA
Verkhoyansk
Kolyma
Tiksie
Petropavlovsk
30°
INTERNATIONAL DATE LINE
40°
50°
60°
70°
Aleutian Islands
Bering Sea
Anadyr
NORTHERN SEA ROUTE
150° EAST
Chukotsk Peninsula
Cape Dezhnev
Little Diomede
Big Diomede
Seward Pen.
BERING STRAIT
MILES
0
50
100
SEE INSET
180°
80° NORTH
INT'L. DATE LINE
Polar
NOR
Pacific Ocean
ALASKA
Seward
Fairbanks
Yukon
150° WEST
Beaufort Sea
120°
90°
BANKS I.
Stefansson I.
MAGNETIC POLE
VICTORIA ISLAND
Mackenzie
ARCTIC CIRCLE
Boothia Pen.
BAFFIN ISLA
Bylo Island
AIRBA
Roes Welcome Sd.
Hudson Bay
Hudson
Pangni
Ungava Peninsula
Belcher Is.
James Bay
Burnt Cre
Los Angeles
Winnipeg
NORTH AMERICA
SOUTHERN LIMIT OF PERMAFRO
Seven Isla
Richard E. Harrison 1956

HERE IS THE FAR NORTH
by
Evelyn Stefansson
0 300 600 900
ORTHOGRAPHIC PROJECTION
MILES
SCALE CORRECT ONLY ALONG PARALLELS
ARCTIC CIRCLE
Yenisei
Ob
Irtysh
Igarka
Norilsk
Taz
Mangazeya
SOUTHERN LIMIT OF PERMAFROST
Taz Bay
Yamal Pen.
Dikson I.
Vorkhuta
Yugorski Shar
Barents Sea
Archangel
White Sea
Murmansk
Leningrad
EUROPE
LAPLAND
Kiruna
Oslo
Copenhagen
30° EAST
SPITSBERGEN
(SVALBARD)
Sea
MERIDIAN OF GREENWICH 0°
80° NORTH
70°
60°
50°
40°
30°
90°
30° WEST
GREENLAND
King Oscars Fjord
Mesters Vig
ICELAND
SEE INSET
Holsteinsborg
BW8
Søndrestrøm Fjord
Strait
Ivigtut
Cape Farewell
Atlantic Ocean
Hamilton Inlet
Goose Bay
Gander
NEWFOUNDLAND
ICELAND
Grimsey
Eyjafjordur
Hallormstadir
Akureyri
Vatnajökull
Lang jökull
Mt. Hekla
Denmark Strait
Keflavik
Reykjavik
MILES
0 100 200

and peculiarities of radio reception seem, alas, to be uniformly encountered. The Eskimo language, despite minor dialect differences and the huge distances that sometimes separate one group of Eskimos from another, is basically the same tongue from Siberia to Greenland. Permafrost is so extensive throughout the North that its southern boundary is often used to define the southern boundary of the sub-Arctic.

Permafrost, or perennially frozen subsoil, is one of the family of arctic phenomena new to most northern tourists. Where it occurs, only a layer of the topsoil above it thaws in summer; below that, it remains frozen hard as concrete the year round. The depth of permafrost may range from a few inches to 2,000 feet, but whether the layer is thick or thin, it effectively prevents underground drainage. Because rain and surface waters cannot penetrate downward, they remain on the surface of the ground forming, literally, millions of lakes. Wherever permafrost occurs, and it is estimated that it underlies one-fifth of the land of the world, the landscape has a typical permafrost look. When you peer downward from a plane and see country where more

Coastline of East Greenland about 280 miles north of Angmagssalik at the most ice-free time of year.

than half of the land is made up of innumerable lakes of every size and shape, the chances are good that permafrost lies below it.

Paleontologists, the scientists who study animal and vegetable life of ages earlier than our own, have reason to be grateful when they discover permafrost. For it provides them with an enormous deep-freeze museum which captured and perfectly preserved the mammoths and other ancient animals that roamed the earth tens of thousands of years ago. Vegetation which may now be extinct, but once flourished as food for the mammoth, has been discovered too. In Alaska, for instance, more than twenty species of mammals, including what we think of as tropical sorts, like camels and elephants, have been dug up, thawed out and studied. Siberia's permafrost has presented us with huge tusked mammoths, some with the meat still edible and hair still intact, although they perished many thousands of years ago!

In addition to supplying marvelous paleontological specimens, permafrost provides some headaches too, especially for engineers and building contractors. For when the topsoils that cover it are removed, and the sun or other heat permitted to touch its frozen area, it thaws, often with painful results. A building whose foundations are set in rock-hard permafrost will now shift crazily, if the normal winter heating of the structure is allowed to penetrate downward. Or a nicely leveled road will develop symptoms resembling the aftermath of a volcanic eruption, if the hot summer sun going to work on its dark surface thaws the permafrost that lies below. The problems of construction in permafrost country are gradually being solved, usually by preventing the thawing of the frost by insulation. If this is done, it remains concrete-like and can actually be a help in construction rather than a hindrance. But let us get back to our transpolar flight—our permafrost side trip has been long enough.

At Winnipeg we changed crews, and in addition to a full complement of officers two extra men came aboard. These were the navigators who would be responsible for guiding us across the relatively unexplored aerial paths that lay ahead. From here on out ground aids to navigation, like radar, would be few and far between. As we left Winnipeg, heading northeastward toward Hudson Bay we encountered the "permafrost look" below for the first time. Innumerable lakes, large and small, highlighted by the early morning sun and reflecting the lovely pinks of dawn, stretched endlessly across the flat prairie landscape.

Now we reached *The Bay*, largest inland water mass in North America, some 900 miles long. Since 1670, when the Hudson's Bay Company was first granted an exclusive royal charter for trading in the bay and along the waters draining into it, Hudson Bay has been *the* bay. Blinding sunshine was reflected from the startling white shore ice, which in winter may extend outward from the land as much as sixty or seventy miles,

The Hudson's Bay Company's second oldest trading post at Moose Factory was established in 1674.

capturing the offshore islands and holding them fast until spring. Now, in May, it was narrower; and beyond it, circles of "pancake" ice looking for all the world like thousands of frosted pancakes, crowded tightly along the edge, gradually thinning out until there was more blue water than cakes.

Compared to the Polar Sea, much of which is 12,000 feet deep, Hudson Bay is shallow, averaging only 70 fathoms, or 420 feet. Until recently it was believed that the bay never froze over entirely, but scientists have now found that it sometimes does. Bay ice is produced locally each winter and most of it is gone by the end of June, except the pressured slabs heaped high by gales, which survive even into late July in the southernmost part of the bay.

As we neared the center of the bay, ice floes scattered and soon we came to open water of a stunning pure hue. Suddenly and poignantly I was reminded that about this time of year (actually in late June) Henry Hudson had perished in these waters, perhaps in this very spot, more than 300 years ago. He was set adrift with a few loyal crewmen in a small boat (for some reason I remember it was called a shallop) by mutineers. With his young son John, who had accompanied him on all his famous voyages, at his side, his boat moved into the unknown and was never seen again by Europeans.

Leaving Hudson Bay and sad thoughts of Henry, we crossed the tip of Ungava Peninsula. Farther south in this land, on the Quebec-Labrador border, a spectacular discovery of incredibly rich iron ore at a spot called Burnt Creek, is radically changing the face of Canada's sub-Arctic. Until recently it was a wilderness unmarked by a sign of man's activity. Now a 360-mile railroad to carry out the rich ore to Seven Islands on the north shore of the St. Lawrence has been built, virtually from the air. In a country without roads, everything needed for building the railroad was brought in by air ferry. Millions of dollars have already been spent and many more will follow to ease and increase the extraction of ore from the open pit mines and send it on its way to the ends of the earth.

Ore began moving out in 1954, with high expectations of

soon reaching the 20 million ton a year goal. Other good mineral possibilities are known from the Ungava Bay region, in the Belcher Islands in Hudson Bay, and in Bylot Island, north of Baffin. A decade ago few would have credited the possibility of developing mineral resources on an economic scale as far north as Burnt Creek. Another decade may see the same thing happening in still higher Canadian latitudes. In arctic lands across the Polar Sea from Canada it happened long ago. In Kiruna in Swedish Lapland, in Spitsbergen, and more recently throughout the Soviet Arctic.

Cruising along at 300 miles an hour we cross Hudson Strait. The land has been gradually changing from prairie to rocky hills. Now we are face to face with jagged peaks and bold, dramatic mountains. Smooth-topped glaciers line the valleys between the heights, twisting and turning, whitely marking the sloping paths down to the sea. And now not only the glaciers are whitened, but mountain tops, too, are powdered with snow although it is almost summer. There is no mistaking this stark and gorgeous land; this is Baffin Island.

William Baffin, whose name was given to this queen of the Canadian Arctic Archipelago, is known as an "explorer's explorer," for those who have followed in his footsteps and studied his careful writings, appreciate his genius. His 1616 voyage explored the bay north of Davis Strait, which also bears his name, and reached a farthest north that was not bettered for 236 years. And it was made in the tiny 55-ton *Discovery* through largely unexplored, ice-filled waters. History knows Baffin only during the last ten years of his life, but how richly he filled the decade which began in 1612! During that short span he made seven important voyages, touching Greenland, Spitsbergen, Hudson Strait and Baffin Bay. On his last voyage he took part in a sea battle and the contemporary account says he was "slaine in fight with a shot as hee was trying his mathematicall projects and conclusions," and "fell gloriously in the service of his country."

Baffin's island is fifth largest in the world, fourth if you count Greenland a continent rather than an island, as some do.

Only Greenland, New Guinea, Borneo and Madagascar outrank in size Baffin Island's 201,600 square miles. It is twice the size of Great Britain.

In 1576 when Queen Elizabeth waved good-bye to Martin Frobisher as he set off to discover the Northwest Passage, the exploration of Baffin Island was begun. Frobisher, who was later knighted for his part in defeating the Spanish Armada, thought he had discovered a passage through Baffin Island, and it was named Frobisher Strait. He was diverted from further attempts at the Northwest Passage by the supposed discovery of gold on the shores of his strait. Plans to develop the mines took precedence over the passage, since they promised a more immediate financial return for the merchants who had financed Frobisher. Sir Martin commanded two more expeditions, the last of which left England to colonize this remote Meta Incognita, and establish a mine. But the gold proved to be "fool's gold," or iron pyrites, and the little colony, so precariously established on the edge of the unknown world, salvaged what men and materials they could and returned home. To complete the sad picture, even Frobisher Strait eventually turned out to be a bay!

Almost 400 years elapsed before the next colonization of Frobisher Bay was attempted. This time the motive was war rather than gold, when in 1942 a weather station and then an air base was established at the head of the bay. Great difficulties were encountered in the construction of the United States-Canadian base, chiefly because of the turbulent, almost forty-foot tides in the bay and the hazards of getting ships through the bay ice to deliver the heavy machinery and huge quantities of supplies required by a remote military installation. In 1956 the weather station was still being maintained and the air base was still manned but with reduced forces.

New importance was conferred on Frobisher Bay when it became the site of one of the Distant Early Warning, or DEW Line radar stations. It is probably the easternmost point of a 3,000 miles long electronic fence designed to warn North America of the approach of enemy planes. Canada and the United States joined hands and forces in 1955, sending north what was

A Hudson's Bay Company trading post at Frobisher Bay.

undoubtedly the largest group of ships ever to enter the Arctic simultaneously. Not only were ships of every type utilized to send in the huge amounts of needed supplies, but airplanes, barges on the Mackenzie River, and long trains of sledges hauled by tractors, "cat trains," were also called into play. Work began at many points (the number of stations still remains secret) on a line reaching from Baffin Island on the east across northern Canada and Alaska. It is planned to extend the system another 1,100 miles to cover the Aleutian chain as well as northern Alaska.

If you think of the Canadian North as all the land beyond the provinces, north of the 60th parallel, it turns out to be one-third of all Canada. This area of one and a half million square miles comprises the Yukon and the Northwest Territories and is about half the size of the United States. It is inhabited by a mere 25,000 people, less than 10,000 of whom are Eskimos. Surely this is one of the most sparsely populated areas in the entire world.

The average person has a tendency to think of all Eskimos, everywhere, as living in igloos, and to think of igloos only as snowhouses. But in Eskimo the word igloo has the broadest of meanings; it means a temporary or permanent shelter for man or beast, so that while a snowhouse is *one* kind of igloo, so is Grand Central Station, a doghouse, and the Cathedral of St. John the Divine. True, in some areas the Eskimos, possibly imitating the white man, now use the word exclusively for a snowhouse.

It may come as a bit of a shock to some to learn that a hundred years ago at least half of all the Eskimos in the world had

A Canadian Eskimo fishing through the ice, protected by his snow shelter.

never even heard of snowhouses, much less seen or lived in one. No primitive Eskimo in Siberia, Alaska and Labrador ever built a snowhouse as a residence. In Greenland, except for a handful of "Polar Eskimos" in the extreme northwest of that huge island, no Greenlander knew the art. Thanks to movies and books, most modern Eskimos know about them.

Only in the central Canadian Arctic has the snowhouse been used as a regular winter residence, tents being substituted in summertime. As far east as Baffin Island and as far west as the Mackenzie Delta, ancestors of the present-day peoples used snowhouses, and many still have a theoretical knowledge of them. A few still use them in emergencies or when traveling. But the majority live in sod houses, with thick cold-proof walls, with rafters of driftwood or whalebone. Alas, in the more so-called civilized areas, imitation white man's dwellings that resemble shacks more than regular houses have sprung up. Attempting to discourage this latter type of housing, the United States Navy at Point Barrow and the Department of Northern Affairs in Canada have introduced more sensible housing.

The idea of owning one's house is a strange one to a Stone Age Eskimo who always felt a house belonged to anyone as long as he lived in it, but no longer. When a new snowhouse can be built by an experienced man in three quarters of an hour, it can also be abandoned without a qualm after a night's camping. But now many Eskimos earn wages, and working for the white man they have learned to drive tractors and handle complicated machinery. They are also picking up the white man's idea of owning a house.

Tides, which proved such a nuisance in Frobisher Bay, have a tendency to run to extremes in the Arctic. It has been discovered recently that tides in Leaf Bay, Ungava, exceed those in Frobisher Bay and even those in the famous Bay of Fundy. On the other hand the usual tide-producing influences practically vanish at the North Pole and any tides originating in the central Polar Sea can be measured in inches. The miniature tides on the shores of the Arctic Sea are due to winds blowing in the neighborhood rather than to the moon, acting on the Polar Basin itself.

ABOVE *A typical snowhouse encampment by Queen Maud Sea. Caribou antlers are shown in the foreground.* BELOW *A sod house in Greenland.*

The largest inlet on Baffin Island is Cumberland Sound just northward of Frobisher. It, too, was discovered in "Good Queen Bess's glorious days," by John Davis in 1584. Davis was a great pilot, a scientific seaman who wrote books on practical navigation, and grew up in a magnificent period of English naval history with such playmates as Humphrey Gilbert and his half brother Walter Raleigh. Davis thought Cumberland Sound was probably a strait. He described carefully the flora and fauna of its shores.

Pangnirtung, the unofficial "capital" of Baffin Island, used to be the most important native settlement in this area and lies toward the head of Cumberland Sound, on its eastern shore. Here Eskimos still live a fairly primitive hunting life. Seals and fish are the mainstays, and at "Pang" the diet includes the small white whale, or beluga. The little settlement has facilities common to fair-sized Eskimo villages in the Canadian Arctic: a Hudson's Bay Company trading post, a Royal Canadian Mounted Police barracks, and in this case the only hospital in the Canadian Arctic Archipelago, with a single doctor in charge of 300,000 square miles!

During this stretch of our flight I took advantage of the Captain's invitation to visit him and his crew in the forward section of our plane, from which small but strategic spot they governed our flight and our lives. This instrument-crowded nose section of the craft had a wide, curved seamless window with a full 180° horizon and offered up to us what seemed to be the whole arctic world. It was a thrilling sight. The weather was clear with the special new-washed clarity that enables one to see far in all directions. The brilliance of sunlight reflected from sea ice and glacier, and the thin dusting of snow which still clothed the landscape below made one reach hurriedly for dark glasses to relieve the glare. Needing sun glasses in the Arctic was another surprise to my fellow passengers, many of whom were unprepared and had to draw their window shades down. I had read too many narratives of exploration, which described all too vividly the agonies of being snowblind, to have come unprepared.

An Eskimo wearing snow goggles to prevent snow blindness.

As we left a coastline or approached another, we would fly through long ribbons of little white cloudlets which seemed to copy the outline of the coast, and temporarily obscured the view. Then back we would shoot again into the crystalline sunshine.

A dizzying array of dials with sensitive quivering needle indicators, banked the panoramic window above and below, reminding us that they had taken over much of what used to be a pilot's job. Little faces, some black, some white, keeping score for the invisible game of automation. Today a pilot's duty consists largely of watching these dials and making a delicate adjustment or perhaps a life-saving decision on the basis of what they tell him.

Conversing with the Captain of our plane, I traded bits of sixteenth century history about the land we were flying over for details about the pleasures and problems of keeping up a regular civilian schedule while flying a new arctic route. As we looked down 17,000 feet to the earth which lay beneath us like a huge physical map, we saw a particularly spectacular cape at the entrance of Cumberland Sound, where the ice-covered highland of the interior slopes down to a hilly region and then drops steeply into the sea. Cumberland Sound was ice filled, but at the foot of the headland was brilliant blue open water. Although I had never seen it before, I said lightly to the Captain:

"That looks like Cape Mercy."

He reached for his aviation chart, examined it and turned around to me with a surprised look.

"It is," he said, "but how in the world did *you* know?"

I confessed that I "recognized" it from a description I had once written of it during World War II. At that time, as a member of my husband's research staff, I helped prepare *Sailing Directions* of northern waters for the United States Navy Hydrographic Office. I had been assigned the Baffin Island section. Knowing the general area we were flying over, I remembered that although Cumberland Sound is filled with ice until July, a tidal rip at the foot of Cape Mercy keeps ice from forming round it most of the year. Seeing a striking headland, with open water at its base, I had guessed it might be the place Davis had named God's Mercy Cape more than 300 years ago.

Where Baffin Island and Greenland are closest, the southern end of Davis Strait is only 180 miles wide. The Arctic Circle sweeps across the strait here and a submarine ridge extending from Cape Walsingham on Baffin to Holsteinsborg in Greenland makes it the shallowest section as well as the narrowest.

Davis Strait may be narrow, but it marks an important division in the arctic world. It separates northern Canada from its neighbor to the east, Greenland. There are many physical differences between the two countries, but far greater are the man-made differences—government, administration, economy and culture. Eskimos inhabit both shores, but they live differently. Until recently Canada, like the United States, was rather indifferent to her arctic peoples; but Greenland, for more than two hundred years, has had an enlightened policy, probably unique in the history of colonial territories. Denmark's aim from the beginning of her influence, after 1720, was almost the opposite of the usual pattern of colonial exploitation. She tried to bridge the difficult gap between a primitive culture and a so-called civilized one. It was largely a program of education, religious as well as secular; its mistakes were friendly ideas gone awry and the average result far in advance of any other country's. Recently this policy reaped its reward, for when the Greenlanders held their first election they requested that their country be incorporated into Denmark, an act rare in colonial history. Today Greenland is a county of Denmark, with two Greenlandic voting members in the Danish Parliament. Compare this with Alaska, for instance, which, although electing a delegate to the United States Congress, has no real representation. Though the delegate may make speeches, he cannot vote, even though Alaskans pay federal taxes.

Crossing Davis Strait offers another "first" to the new arctic tourist. Here for the first time in our flight we have a good chance of sighting icebergs, in addition to the sea ice, in the waters below. The shallow ridges, offshore islands and shoal places along the coast, all have a tendency to delay icebergs on their regularly scheduled southerly travel route. So they bunch up.

"But icebergs and sea ice—aren't they two ways of saying the same thing? What's the difference, if any?" asked one passenger.

The differences are basic and important. Sea ice is produced by the freezing of *salt* ocean water. Icebergs, although they live in the salt sea, are created on land, from snow. True the snow eventually becomes ice, but it always remains fresh. Sea ice, though originally salty, becomes fresh during its second year.

Icebergs are the children of glaciers, born when a moving river of ice reaches the sea. The birth process, when a chunk breaks off the stiff ice river, is called "calving" and produces thunderous noises and tumultuous waves along with each new berg. There are a few berg-producing glaciers in the Canadian Arctic, but they are negligible compared with Greenland's factory of more than 200 berg-producing glaciers, most of which are offshoots from the tremendous Greenland Ice Cap.

Icebergs may be almost any size, from tiny bits to what has been called a record berg, seven miles long, three and one half miles wide, and fifty feet high. Some rise as high as two or three hundred feet above the waterline and they assume every imaginable shape, depending on their age and the kind of glacier that produced them. Some are worn smooth by constant washing of the sea and develop fantastic shapes that resemble modern sculpture.

While the number of icebergs drifting southward to perish in the warmer southerly waters is small, compared to the amount of sea ice, the few bergs that survive may be dangerous to North Atlantic shipping. Ever since the horrifying tragedy of the *Titanic,* which sank from ramming an iceberg, the United States Coast Guard maintains an Ice Patrol which charts the iceberg areas and broadcasts their probable course.

Forward in the crew's quarters again, we now approached the Greenland coast, always a splendid sight, but today it was dazzling. I had seen this section of Greenland, around Holsteins-

Icebergs off Greenland's rocky coast.

borg, from shipboard as well as from the land during the summer of 1953. From the air the view was like nothing one could imagine unless it be in a dream. Instead of seeing a fraction of one side of a mountain range, eyes could encompass the whole; instead of a patch of fjord, one could see both sides of the entrance, the body and the head. The size and shape of the coast, with its glacier-filled valleys, the live white haze on the horizon announcing the presence of the Inland Ice which holds most of Greenland in its frosty embrace, the bright sunshine and the blue open water, all contrived to give one a consciousness of the texture and grandeur of the arctic world.

Suddenly, with a feeling of recognition and communion, I was reminded of Isak Dinesen's haunting description of flying in a very different part of the world. In her exquisite *Out of Africa* she had written:

"Every time that I have gone up in an aeroplane and looking down have realized that I was free of the ground, I have had the consciousness of a great new discovery. 'I see': I have thought, 'This was the idea. And now I understand everything.' "*

With an effort I pulled myself back to reality and watched the Captain unhook a microphone from the tangle of wires and dials before him. In a quiet voice he called the radio operator at the Bluie West 8 radar base which perches at the head of Sondrestrom Fjord, where we were going to land and refuel. He very kindly plugged in an extra set of earphones and handed them to me so I might eavesdrop on the conversation. Receiving no answer, he paused and repeated his message over again, and then again. From our conversation I knew the Captain would not follow the curving, winding path of the fjord to its head, but would shorten our journey by cutting across the terrifyingly beautiful mountains. Looking down at the snow-covered peaks a realization of our utter helplessness should anything go wrong, passed apprehensively through my mind. As these gloomy thoughts were taking shape an everyday, slightly southern oh-so-American voice answered the Captain's call in a relaxed and cheerful manner, instantly dispelling all possibilities of disaster.

* From Isak Dinesen's *Out of Africa*, Random House, Inc., 1938, 1952. By permission of the publishers.

Like the butler at a formal party, the Captain announced us. The invisible radio voice acknowledged the introduction and began to guide us toward an equally invisible landing field. It told us when to change our course, how many degrees to shift, at what speed to approach the field, at what altitude, and at the very moment it said "your wheels should touch the runway," they did, with the nose of the plane smack on the yellow stripe marking the center of the field. A perfect landing north of the Arctic Circle!

Navigators in the Arctic, more than in other parts of the world, hold the safety of an airplane and its passengers in their hands.

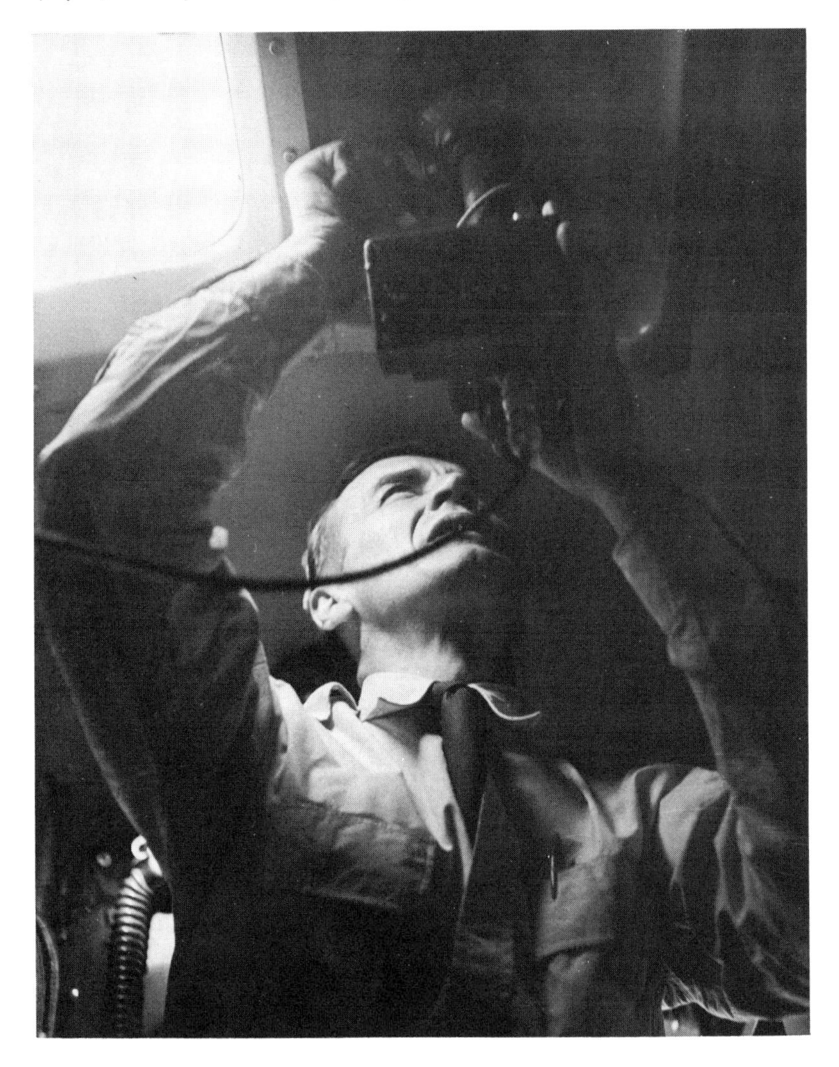

With the first response of the radio voice I could almost feel the relaxation of tension to my right, where the two navigators were working. They had been far too busy from the moment we left Winnipeg even to look up from their work as I went in and out of their quarters and brushed past their cramped working space. Now they laid down earphones, slide rules and dividers and for the first time stretched and started moving about. For the moment, their work was done, but on long arctic flights these men are the busiest and in some ways the most important members of the crew.

Manuals tell us that air navigation is "the art of conducting an aircraft from place to place whether or not the ground is observed, by day or night." A navigator must know where he is, in what direction he is heading, and how to stay on his determined course. Under ideal conditions it requires a clear head and good training; in the Arctic certain unusual conditions conspire to make his task especially difficult.

The magnetic compass has been the mainstay of European travelers since around 1300; the Chinese are said to have known it as early as 300 A.D. Due to the presence in Canada of the North Magnetic Pole, which is a gently shifting area moving within the Arctic, rather than a stationary imaginary pin point like the North Pole, the magnetic compass on our route becomes weak, unreliable and practically useless. The gyro compass has been substituted, but it too is subject to error which must be calculated often and regularly—sometimes requiring the full-time services of one navigator. New types of compasses are being developed now especially for northern flying. One of these is the polarized light compass which spots the sun even when it is below the horizon, an important factor in arctic flying during the sunless winter days.

Twilight is the least favorable time of day, from a navigator's point of view, because then he has neither sun nor stars with which to check his position. In temperate zones this is a relatively short period. In the tropics the shift from day to night is swift and twilight hardly exists at all, but in the Arctic it poses a serious problem, for it can last for *days*. On an east-west flight in the higher latitudes a plane cannot only keep up with the sun, but may overtake it and have to fly indefinitely in a condition of twilight.

Another problem to plague northern navigators is that, on moving into high latitudes, map projections like the Mercator on which they ordinarily plot their courses become less and less useful, because of the sphericity of the earth and the gathering of the meridians toward the Pole. New projections have had to be devised, and old ones revised, but none is perfect. Strangely enough, when navigating north of 75° N. Latitude, one of the most useful projections is the stereographic which was invented in the second century B.C. by the Greek astronomer Hipparchus! A new method used with some success is a system called Grid Direction which entirely ignores familiar map projections and substitutes instead a network of squares for guide lines instead of meridians and parallels.

Ground aids to navigation, like radio beacons, radar and related inventions, are numerous and taken for granted in the populated section of the world. But in the Arctic, except for the thin line which marks the Distant Early Warning or DEW Line network of stations along North America's northerly coasts, they are practically non-existent. As if all these problems were not sufficient, radio reception in the Arctic is generally poor and uncertain, so the radio signals on which a navigator depends normally are not always available to him. Therefore the navigators on long northern flights, more than in any other part of the world, hold the safety and destiny of plane and passengers in their hands as they measure, plot, map and check. It may not be long before their job becomes like the pilot's, semi-automatic with only buttons to push and dials to watch, but meantime they are the busiest men aboard.

As we lost speed, and taxied along the air base runway, a perky little jeep appeared suddenly with a large yellow sign on its back reading "Follow me." Our huge craft meekly trailed the tiny bug of a car until we came to rest finally at the refueling berth. Now for the first time since leaving Winnipeg, half a day before, we could leave the plane, stretch our legs and inspect an arctic air base nestling at the edge of the Greenland Ice Cap. Fine snow was falling, the nippy below-freezing air felt delightfully fresh. A khaki bus came to meet us and carried us to a tiny red Danish "hotel" which looked even smaller than it was because of the huge mountain forming a towering backdrop. Here on the edge of "nowhere" we entered and found a handsome modern restaurant and gift shop, complete with postcards, Greenland handicrafts, Danish silver and porcelain for sale. In less than an hour, after refreshments, shopping and postcard writing, we reboarded the plane. Next stop, Copenhagen, tomorrow morning.

Aloft again there loomed ahead, seemingly larger than life itself, the Ice Cap, or the Inland Ice, or the Greenland Ice Cap, however you choose to address this collossus which defers only to the Antarctic Ice Sheet as the largest glacier in the world. Fifteen hundred miles long, 200 to 500 miles wide—637,000 square miles of fresh, recrystalized ice that once was snow, covering eighty-five per cent of all Greenland.

The Inland Ice is by far the greatest producer of icebergs in the Northern Hemisphere, greater than all others put together. It sends hundreds of outlet glaciers to the north, east and west, pushing beyond the high rugged coastal mountains which contain it. Some of the off-shoot glaciers are narrow, ribbon-like affairs, meeting the sea at the head of some quiet fjord; others, present bold cliff-like faces to the open sea. Then there is the supreme Humboldt Glacier in latitude 80° N., on the west coast, largest of all the outlets with a glittering 60-mile wide front.

In some of the most northerly settlements on Greenland's west coast, iceberg bits from these glaciers supply the only fresh water available to the community for drinking and cooking purposes. In such settlements each house has a huge iron pot atop the stove into which the day's supply is dumped to melt while the meal is cooking.

The Greenland Ice Cap, the second largest glacier in the world.

Sea ice will, of course, become fresh as it ages, but it must be more than a year old before enough salt has been eliminated to make it palatable for drinking and coffee making. Knowledge that salt is removed from sea ice, by the alternate freezing and thawing process it undergoes in the course of a year, was common for centuries. But it was known only to "practical" men—whalers and sealers and those who lived or had spent many winters in the North. Only within this century has the knowledge finally seeped through to oceanographers and other scientists. Salt shore ice formed at the northerly settlements does not last through the summer, or long enough to freshen; so iceberg ice is utilized instead.

Deep below its frosty burden, Greenland is said to be an undulating submerged mountain landscape, some of it depressed by the enormous weight of the ice to *below* sea level. The edge of the Ice Cap is steep and rough where it meets the ice-free land, providing a harsh initiation for those polar explorers who have tried to cross it. These rough outer sections of the ice are scored with deep and dangerous crevasses, the bottomless fractures produced by ice pressures and tensions. When the landscape is snow-covered the mouth of a crevasse may be lightly filled with snow and the presence of the gaping danger cannot be detected except by careful probing and testing.

Throughout Greenland's history, crevasses have exacted a heavy toll of unwary travelers. Men, sleds, dogs, equipment and in more recent times, tractors and snow "weasels," have vanished from sight in an instant, sometimes without a sound, sometimes with a terrible screech of agony. Then silence. Since a crevasse may be as deep as a mile, it is needless to say that there are few survivors. If the crevasse be shallow, and a man is not alone, or not injured too badly, he may survive, and there have been such lucky ones. But more often men and equipment have disappeared without a trace.

Nunataks are snow free mountain peaks which poke their tops through a glacier, and they, too, are encountered on the fringes of the Ice Cap. But, beyond the crevasses and the nunataks, the ice becomes smoother and smoother, eventually being transformed from a place of nightmarish danger into a kind of heavenly white sparkling highway with no visible boundaries. It slopes ever so gently upward from the west coast and then downward to the east. This is the area where a plane can land easily. Some explorers crossing this part of the Cap have literally sailed along, for they made canvas sails for their sledges which caught the winds and made them speed across the white desert.

Fridtjof Nansen, the great Norwegian who may be termed the "perfect explorer," was the first to cross the Ice Cap. He did it in 1888 with five young and husky companions, all of them expert skiers; *he* was a champion. Nansen brought many talents to his distinguished career as an explorer. He was a first-class zoologist and oceanographer, an inventor, writer, historian and artist.

Nansen's Ice Cap expedition, despite the most discouraging beginnings and unforeseen difficulties that would have turned other men homeward, was his first great success and made him

In northerly Greenland settlements glacier ice is gathered by dog team to be melted down for drinking water. This picture was taken in Holsteinsborg, north of Sondrestrom Fjord.

an international hero. Armed with youth, health, high spirits and their battle cry "Death or the west coast," it is hard to see how they could have failed, but many before them had. The work of Nansen, Otto Sverdrup and their companions, destroyed many myths about the Inland Ice and secured priceless meteorological information. Most important, perhaps, was that it started Nansen on a career fated to be one of the longest and most glorious chapters in the history of northern exploration.

In later life Nansen was even more of a hero than in his youth. Working with the League of Nations, it was he who designed the Nansen Passport which offered hope and life to thousands of homeless unfortunates following World War I. Between 1917 and 1920 almost a million and a half political refugees fled from Russia alone. All were without passports or citizenship papers and therefore were unable to travel from one country to another. In 1922, Nansen designed the certificate which gave them League of Nations "citizenship" and coaxed fifty nations into agreeing to honor the substitute passes. Exiles at last were able to seek new homes, obtain work, collect their scattered families and retrieve what was left of their shattered lives.

Nansen's selfless work and utter sincerity conferred on him a kind of international diplomatic immunity. He moved freely across hostile borders. Everyone trusted him. A colleague said of him that "there was not a country in Europe where wives and mothers have not wept in gratitude" for his work.

As we flew so comfortably across the Ice Cap, I drank a silent toast to the men who preceded Nansen, and to those that followed and still follow. Our own American Peary, the Danish Mylius-Erichsen who perished, as did the German Wegener, the Michigan college professor Hobbs, the modest Englishman Courtauld, and more recently our good French friend Paul-Emile Victor who carries on the noble tradition of pushing back still farther the frontiers of ignorance. It is a tradition which has included men from many nations and many professions.

A scientific laboratory cut right into the Greenland Ice Cap.

The island country immediately eastward of Greenland, actually within sight from her eastern coast on a clear day, is more than any other in the North, a romantic, story-book sort of land. The ancients called it "Ultima Thule," the farthest land; we call it Iceland. It contains both glaciers and active volcanoes, in some places actually side by side, and hot springs abound throughout its countryside.

We know Iceland's history at first vaguely, from when the Greek philosopher-explorer Pytheas told of it about 300 years B.C. We know it with strange precision from the moment in 874 A.D. when the Scandinavians began colonizing it. Their descendants, the present-day Icelanders, Irish and Norse in nearly equal proportions, are a most interesting and unusual people; according to some writers, unique. Numbering only 160,000, they are the most literate people in the world. Icelanders today produce more poets and prose writers, buy, sell and read more books per capita, than any other peoples. They have won Nobel prizes in medicine and literature, and many of their names are internationally known in the fields of art and music. Icelanders have always been interested in poetry, geneology and history. Long before the famous Icelandic Sagas were written down they were recited to audiences large and small by talented speakers. To this day many Icelanders can recite long passages from them by heart.

These traits are all the more remarkable when one remembers that four-fifths of Iceland consists of desert, unfit for human habitation. The desert is of two types: ice desert, created by huge glaciers, and lava desert, the handiwork of numerous volcanic eruptions. Then, too, Iceland's climate which is never very cold and never very hot, is not sufficiently warm to ripen cereal crops. No natural resources of any consequence are to be found within the country.

Fifty to a hundred years ago Iceland was one of the poorest, most backward and disease-ridden countries in the world. Her history up to that time had been marred by earthquake, volcanic eruption, starvation and plague, which had decimated her ranks and devastated the countryside. Today Iceland is one of the healthiest countries in the world. Her people are prosperous, well dressed, well educated, and live in attractive modern homes. Her farms are mechanized and electrified; the standard of living is high. Despite their small numbers, Icelanders support a modern university; a National Library, Museum, Theatre; art museums and numerous other cultural facilities unexpected in so small a country. This striking transformation has all taken place in the last fifty years and until recently without any outside help.

Since there were no resources within the country to exploit, the Icelanders looked beyond their shores and discovered the rich fishing waters that surround them. Fish now supply her main export and dollar-sterling income. Icelanders harnessed their hot springs by piping the water to heat the hothouses which grow the vegetables and flowers they cannot raise outdoors. The

A village in Iceland. On the right is Vilhjalmur Stefansson, the author's explorer husband.

swimming pool that is part of every school in the land is heated by volcanic water. Most of the hot water for laundry purposes, both in town and country, comes from the same source. Now even the capital city of Reykjavik heats the homes of its 70,000 inhabitants with volcanic hot water piped from miles outside the town, and Iceland no longer needs to import expensive coal.

Climatically speaking, Iceland is not an arctic country at all; only its little offshoot of Grimsey, off the northern coast, is north of the Circle. But her close connection with Greenland, both geographically and historically, and her special physical conditions, draw her toward the arctic orbit, although strictly speaking she is in the sub-Arctic. She is also part of the Western Hemisphere, as Lincoln's Secretary of State, Seward, pointed out—she lies on the American side of the Atlantic and is much closer to Greenland than to the nearest European land.

Iceland was colonized in the ninth century by Norwegian expatriates who left their country rather than bow to King Harald the Fairhaired, the first ruler to unite the numerous small kingdoms of Norway under a single head. The unification was not well received by the smaller, less powerful earls and princes, most of whom preferred to rule themselves than be ruled by another. With their families, slaves, and most of their goods, they moved into France to become the Normans, conquered and ruled parts of England and Ireland, and came to Iceland. When they arrived, they found already in residence Irish priests, some of them married, who had sought solitude and a contemplative holy life in Thule. When the Norsemen arrived, most of the religious men fled. But Iceland's history has lured us off our transpolar course; let us return.

Flying over Iceland the glaciers are clearly marked, especially those that lie beside the mat black lava deserts, which seem to absorb all color and form, producing an eerie shadowless landscape. The coasts of the fjord-indented shores are brilliant green in summer with lush, thick grass which has been compared favorably with the green sod of Ireland. Like Greenland's shores, Iceland's rise steeply from the sea to present a striking profile; and, also like that larger country, Iceland is now almost treeless, but in ancient times it was wooded.

When we left the head of Sondrestrom Fjord, we flew eastward and then southeastward across Iceland. Once Iceland is past, we are again in familiar waters as we approach Scotland and the North Sea. With morning we arrive at Copenhagen's airport, having glimpsed a new portion of the earth.

The polar world, already explored by the scientists, is waiting to be discovered by the tourist. Besides permafrost, glaciers and sea ice, it contains grass-covered prairie, wild flowers and minerals to be discovered. Besides air bases, weather stations and radar beacons, there are cities waiting to be built as the resources are developed. Here is the last frontier for a crowded northern people.

But flying over a country at 300 miles an hour is far too swift for getting anything but a quick impression; and quick impressions have a way of proving untrue, since they are only small segments of a much larger canvas. So we return to the countries we sped across at such a pace for a more leisurely look at the land, the people and their way of life.

II

Greenland:

DENMARK'S NEWEST COUNTY

Igaliko, a modern settlement in West Greenland, also flourished a thousand years ago in Erik the Red's time.

ONE
The Land, the Climate and the Greenlanders

ON A chilly New York City day of November, 1954, in the skyscraper palace housing the United Nations, two quietly dressed, soft spoken gentlemen rose to address a gathering and created a singular moment in political history. It is unlikely, even if you looked sharply at the speakers, that you could guess their nationality correctly. Some might call them Eskimos, but they and their people prefer, quite rightly, to be addressed as Greenlanders. Their names were Aage Lynge and Frederik Lynge, and their home—the largest island in the world, and they were brand new members of the Danish Parliament. They had been democratically elected the summer of 1953 in the first general election of its kind ever held in Greenland.

When Greenland came of age after centuries of Danish colonial rule, instead of demanding full independence in the usual manner of non-self-governing territories, she actually asked to be *joined* with Denmark, calling it her mother country. This dramatic merger had already taken place at the time of the U.N. meeting, and the appearance of the Greenlanders in New York was in the nature of both a "hail and farewell."

Instead of a colony, Greenland was now officially a county of Denmark—the largest county in the world, many times bigger than Texas. Her two spokesmen enjoyed complete equality with other members of the Royal Danish Parliament to give voice to their problems and opinions. Greenlanders were increasingly taking over the administration and government of their own country. Now that Greenland was an integral part of the Danish Realm she would no longer have to report to the U.N. Committee on Information from Non-Self Governing Territories—this was the final report.

Stretching backward from this moving ceremony was a pattern, centuries in the making, of an enlightened and unselfish Danish policy which made it all possible. It had been, since 1720, an administration so successful it might be used as a model by other countries called on to govern a colony with few resources and a population of so-called "uncivilized" folk. It is rare, perhaps especially in the political world, that virtue is rewarded. Experience has shown that it takes a delicate combination of knowledge, understanding, patience and good humor on the part of a donor to permit a less educated people to accept money and services without resentment and even hatred. This, not-very-rich Denmark accomplished gloriously.

That Denmark succeeded is all the more remarkable when you examine geographically the land she had to work with. Greenland is a huge country, 840,000 square miles. Translated into more familiar terms it is about the size of that part of the United States east of the Mississippi. While representing the exception rather than the rule in arctic geography, Greenland comes close to the average man's conception of what *all* far northern countries are like.

The island bears the largest ice cap in the Northern Hemisphere. This is not just a large glacier, but a veritable continent of ice, second in size only to the vast Antarctic Ice Sheet. It smothers eighty-five per cent of Greenland's land surface and is more than two *miles* deep in places. By usually accepted theory, its incredible weight depresses the land to more than a thousand feet below sea level in some places; in others, the mountain peaks rise 10,000 feet above the sea, their tops peeking up through the ice.

Greenland's length is 1,600 miles, from the northernmost cape in the world, within 440 miles of the North Pole, to well south of the Arctic Circle. Its southern tip lies in the same latitude as Seward, Alaska; Oslo, Norway; and Leningrad, in the Soviet Union. The giant Inland Ice permits only a narrow strip of land along the coastline to slip through its frosty fingers. Nowhere on the west coast is this strip wider than a hundred

The harbor of Godhavn, Disko Island, Greenland.

miles. In many places it dwindles to nearly or quite nothing. Fjords cut deeply into the land, often to the face of the Ice Cap, further subtracting from the comparatively small, habitable area. In this narrow, rocky, ice-free belt, grassy and flower-strewn in summer, live the Greenlanders.

Settlements are sprinkled at intervals along the western shore from Kap Farvel (Cape Farewell) to northward beyond the United States Thule Air Base, to a place called Kranak, or Thule village. Here at the most northerly settlement live 400 Greenlanders, the last remnants of the Polar Eskimos. They used to live near the airfield, but the noise of jet planes taking off and landing at the American-built NATO Base frightened away the animal life. Or at least that is what they believed. For this and other reasons, the settlement was moved northward. Except for this new settlement and the servicemen manning the base, who are never counted in the population figures, all Greenlanders live south of the parallel 75° North. Sixteen hundred Greenlanders dwell in the two large villages on the east coast, but here, too, the modern world has intruded. Lead deposits, rich enough to develop for commercial purposes, were discovered at Mesters Vig on this even more sparsely populated coast and are now being exploited.

This might be an appropriate place to explain why the Greenlanders want to be called Greenlanders rather than Eskimos. Principally it is because it is the more accurate term. All Greenlanders were once Eskimo, but they have been mixing their blood with Europeans for almost a thousand years. Probably from the time of Erik the Red and his fellow-Scandinavians, who colonized the land in the tenth century, and certainly since the sixteenth century when whalers of many nationalities began to touch Greenland shores, there has been a blending. Today it is not at all uncommon to meet blond, blue-eyed Greenlanders, who speak only the Eskimo language and retain many Eskimo ways. The laws of genetics insist that if four of Mongol (or Eskimo) types marry four blonds, the dark traits will dominate. In the first generation all children will have eyes of the brown Mongol-Eskimo color. In later generations if they have four

Three Greenlanders.

children each, three will be dark-eyed and dark-haired, only one blond. Therefore the blond part of the mixture is greater than is immediately apparent. Probably only a handful of "pure" Eskimos are left in Greenland today.

Some 24,000 Greenlanders then make up the bulk of the country's people. About 1,500 Danish engineers, civil servants, educators and technical experts complete the picture. In theory, and generally in practice, the Danes have no feeling of racial superiority to complicate their relations with the Greenlanders. This may be an important reason for their happy relationship.

The Danish constitutional changes which recently transformed the political status and structure of Greenland, form only one of several major changes which have been occurring simultaneously. The second change, and the one with the greatest physical impact, has been the recent gradual warming of the Greenland climate. You might think that the warming of a "harsh polar climate" would be a great boon, something to be welcomed joyously by the entire population. But the actual effect was the opposite, and except for action taken by the government, could have resulted in disaster.

As Greenland waters became warmer, the sea ice which normally closed in a good portion of the coast, began to retreat farther and farther northward. Here the armchair explorer can almost be heard congratulating nature for improving matters and bestowing the gifts of added warmth and comfort on the Greenlanders. But in the past, along with the sea ice, came food in the shape of seal, walrus and whale. Without the protection of the ice floes, to which they were accustomed, fewer sea mammals visited the coast, and those that came were harder to secure.

Here was tragedy for the Greenlander. Not only was he deprived of food, but the same event also robbed him of both light and heat. The blubber of the great beasts had been burned in lamps to cook the food, warm the house and shed a soft and pleasing light within, throughout the many long twilight nights. Worst of all, there was now no material with which to fashion the remarkable Eskimo skin clothing, which more than anything else had permitted him to live vigorously, in mobile comfort, through otherwise impossibly cold winters.

There was a silver lining to the cloud of Greenland's warming up. While the warmer waters succeeded in keeping away the sea mammals, they also attracted valuable fish that had never before advanced as far north as Greenland. Chief among these was the cod.

But the way of life that supports a seal-, whale- and walrus-hunting economy is not well suited to one which depends for survival on cod fishing. And this brings us to the third great change taking place in modern Greenland—the shift from a self-sufficient hunting mode of existence to a complicated "money economy." The requirements for success in these two types of cultures are so different it is easy to visualize the difficulties and heart break involved in the shift, however gradual it may be.

A hunting village is of necessity small. The equipment

needed for securing food animals is relatively simple and completely homemade. If the hunting season is good, a man and his family are well off—they have food, clothing, housing and shipping. They need nothing and ask little from the civilized world.

On the other hand, the requirements for a successful cod fishery are entirely different. Communities *must* be larger. Bigger and heavier boats are needed. They must venture farther out into the ocean than the beautiful Eskimo skin kayak or umiak, however skillfully made, can manage. Then the catch must be salted or canned or quick-frozen. Machinery enters the picture now—motors for boats, freezing and canning equipment for the factories. Mass produced imports are now a necessity.

Money, a commodity unknown to the old-time hunter, is needed by the Greenlander who wants to take part in this new way of life. He is no longer self-sufficient.

Now he must borrow money to buy his boat, for its lumber is imported, and while he is a mechanical wonder when it comes to repairing the motor, he cannot build one from scratch. He needs gear for the boat, nets, sails and food for the journey out. Now he must buy his clothes, since codfish skins are not suitable for winter clothing, and again he needs money. In the old days a man's wife could dress him from head to foot, making his mittens and waterproof boots as well as his trousers and coats. Then she had both the leisure and the educated skill. Now, the chances are, she has neither. She may be employed in one of the freezing plants, at the local school or hospital or bakery, and if she still makes her family's clothes, she makes them of imported cotton and wool (often in a tartan pattern), and sews them on an imported sewing machine, all of which requires money.

Throughout this period of change the Danish government has played an admirable role. They financed and built the freezing and canning plants; sent technical experts to instruct and train the Greenlanders in their use. They loaned money on easy terms to enterprising fishermen, enabling them to purchase their own boats and equipment. They sent hundreds of Greenlanders to Denmark for special education, all designed to help them to help themselves and take their rightful place in a modern world. This was done in addition to regular long-range programs designed to provide Greenlanders with improved general education, medical facilities and housing, and to raise the standards of their agriculture and sheep farming.

Scientists are agreed that our climate is becoming warmer but that its warming and cooling is a matter of cycles. Long cycles involving thousands of years, like those that produced our former Ice Ages, and shorter ones of dozens rather than thousands of years. Few, however, are agreed on the causes of these fluctuations. Explanations range from sun spots to glacial action. Some think we are now in the midst of a long cycle; others, that this is only a short one. A prominent M.I.T. professor predicts, on the basis of sunspots, that we are about to enter on a reversal of the present trend and the immediate future will be considerably colder. A marine biologist friend of mine uses certain lowered arctic water temperatures as evidence for the same theory. A few say they just don't know, others take a wait-and-see attitude, still others think it will get warmer before it gets colder. A genuine reversal of the climate trend would certainly threaten the hard-won gains of the Greenlanders.

Until 1953, Greenland was a closed country, as much a forbidden land as Tibet. No one entered unless he could show that his coming would benefit the Greenlanders, and even if he could he still had to obtain permission and take a physical examination. The main reason for this restriction was that in Greenland, as well as everywhere else in the Arctic, it had been tragically demonstrated that when white men entered the country they carried diseases to which the ancestors of the natives had never been exposed. They were therefore extremely susceptible and died in terrible numbers from what we are used to thinking of as mild diseases—influenza, whooping cough and measles. Now the worst scourge of all is tuberculosis, a serious illness still with us, but devastating to the Greenlanders.

We and our ancestors have had these diseases for thousands of years. Those who were specially susceptible died long ago; those who survived produced children who inherited their im-

ABOVE *Farming scene in southwestern Greenland.* BELOW *Greenland sheep farmers usually live inland, often at the heads of the fjords, but sheep are also seen in the small coastal fishing villages.*

munity. This gives us automatically what the medical people call "inherited immunity" and that is what primitive man, wherever he dwelt, lacked. No ancient Eskimo ever had the measles and when it first spread like wildfire, whether in Alaska or Greenland, or the South Seas, it wiped out the majority of the population. In one Alaskan village it is said to have killed ninety-nine per cent of the natives!

Long before we had our present concept of germ warfare, white men were killing off the North American Indian and Eskimo with just such a weapon, unconsciously, of course. This type of "warfare" was not limited to North America, or indulged in only by our countrymen. It happened throughout the world in every age, whenever "civilized" man met with "primitive" man—except, of course, in disease-ridden continents like Africa and Asia.

Another aspect of Greenland's closed country policy was that it prevented the exploitation of the local people by dishonest traders, who in other northern countries were quick to take advantage of the good-natured, hospitable, well-mannered but unsophisticated Eskimo.

So one formerly had to be something like a geologist, or a medical man, or a civil servant, anthropologist, writer or oceanographer to obtain a permit to enter Greenland. But in 1953, in accord with the wish of the Greenlanders that they become a part of the Danish Realm, it was felt that the closed country policy was beginning to be outdated, and some thought it unrealistic. Sooner or later it would have to be abandoned, and if Greenland was to enjoy the many advantages of being part of the Western World, she would have to suffer the misfortunes as well.

Today anyone may visit Greenland, at least theoretically. The temporary difficulty is one of obtaining transportation. For Greenland is having a building boom; the ships are crowded, the passenger space scarce and at a premium, with priority given naturally to engineers and carpenters rather than to tourists. The hotels are almost non-existent. Nevertheless there is much talk of a tourist trade for the future. Flying over Greenland has become a commonplace, everyday affair. The gossip includes summer cruises, the building of luxury hotels and summer skiing resorts. And why not? The scenery is about the most gorgeous in the world, the people are little known and fascinating, and the very fact that it has been a closed country for so long should prove one of the strongest tourist attractions!

Flying over Greenland in winter, it seems a vast mountain-bordered snow desert which harbors no living thing. From 17,000 feet above there is no hint that man has ever even stepped ashore on its soil, or that any animal, large or small, ever survived, much less was born within its empty-seeming borders. A thin powder of snow envelops the landscape as late as May or even June, depending on latitude, presenting a gleaming, painfully white surface to the eye, revealing only broad outlines with little or no detail. All color comes from outside the land itself. Blues, soft and harsh, reflected from the sky or surrounding waters, rosy rich hues from sunrise or sunset, and the many colored brilliances of the Northern Lights—all are flashed back and forth again and again from one snow crystal to another forming endless variations on the white.

But fly low over Greenland in summer and a different world welcomes you. A world that has borrowed the entire spectrum of an artist's palette. The mountains seem to have developed personality, for they are varied in shape and as colorful as the national dress of the Greenlandic women. Rugged and smooth, jagged-toothed or smoothly eroded, they appear blue and purple and pink and grey. At their feet nestles a bright green border of grass. Lichens tint the rocks with subtle, ancient colors, and brilliant flowering plants of magenta, yellow and white scatter their color through the grass, often taking over an entire hillside.

Valley glaciers, offshoots of the Inland Ice, neatly fill the low places between many of the mountains. Unless you look carefully, these can scarcely be distinguished from the rest of the landscape in winter. But in summer the glaciers twinkle and shine in the sunlight. Their borders are sharply defined; their color contrasts strikingly with the grassy, hummocky landscape. Now it is easy to see where they begin, where they are going and where they end. One can see them discharge their icebergs quietly at the head of some fjord, or dump them without ceremony, and with lots of crashing noises, into the ocean waters of Baffin Bay.

Presently a settlement appears, precariously perched at the edge of a steep mountain. Its little modern houses, arranged without pattern, are painted bright red, blue, yellow and green, and catch the sun like a handful of uncut jewels carelessly thrown down the stony slopes, and have come to rest at different levels.

Alight at the settlement. Walk about. If you are in southern Greenland, the houses will have carefully tended flower and vegetable gardens, the latter with cold frames to protect them from early frosts. Farther north one sees many little hothouses attached to one end of a regular dwelling, probably for reasons of warmth, economy and convenience, and here both vegetables and flowers bloom in profusion. Southward-facing windows in almost every house are tenanted by tomato, parsley and lettuce plants in addition to the usual flowering ones. The Danish people are extraordinarily fond of house plants, no home in Denmark being considered "dressed" without a supply, artistically arranged, and religiously tended. The Greenlanders were quick to borrow the custom. It is a delightful surprise to enter some tiny home, far north of the Arctic Circle, where the local outdoor vegetation is sparse, and be greeted by a sunburst of colored plants arranged with cunning design.

Suppose now it is a holiday, say the King's birthday, or the arrival of some distinguished visitor that is being celebrated. Then the Greenlanders will don their national costume. The women's dress is more colorful and costly than the men's, and includes many more items, all of them handmade.

Short sealskin trousers with the fur outside are trimmed with strips of colored and sometimes embroidered leather. They are joined in mid-thigh by the tops, sometimes furred, of beautiful, long leather *kamiks,* or boots. These are smooth, the fur having been scraped off, and are gleaming white or bright red when worn by children and young girls. The married women choose blue and other more conservative colors. Stretching from their

ABOVE *One of the innumerable flowering plants that grow north of the Circle. These are showy and "form large flat cushions, often many feet in diameter."*
BELOW *A visit from the Prime Minister of Denmark is being celebrated. Icelandic ponies may be seen in the foreground.*

black soles to well above the knee, these boots give the females an attractive long-legged look, whatever their age. The upper part of the costume consists of a patterned long-sleeved cotton blouse, anchored at the natural waistline by a wide cummerbund of checked or striped taffeta ribbon. Atop the blouse is the most important item of all. This is a large multi-colored, cape-like collar reaching almost to the waist, made entirely of beads, or "pearls" as they are called locally. The heavy beaded openwork is hung from a stiff black stand-up fur collar which encircles the neck loosely, for it is wide enough to slip easily over the head. Bashful children, as well as older girls interested in flirting, find it a useful screen behind which to hide their chins, permitting only a glistening pair of eyes and a tiny nose to show above it.

A man's holiday suit provides a foil to the gaudier female plumage. It consists of only two items—navy or black wool trousers and a spotless white *anorak.* The anorak is a wonderfully becoming long-sleeved shirt with an attached hood, usually worn thrown back to form a kind of collar. Its whiteness frames the tanned faces of the men effectively, and whether or not the hood is in position, it covers the neck up to the chin. In days when seal and caribou were plentiful, the same Eskimo pattern was used for making skin shirts. When white men first introduced woven cloth, Eskimos throughout the Arctic found it useful. They made cotton replicas of their fur garments, and wore them on top of the furs to protect them from rain or snow, both of which soon rot skin clothing unless they are dried quickly.

When the warmer Greenland climate eliminated most of the sea mammals from the coastal waters, and skins for clothing became scarce, wool and cotton materials were substituted, still using the Eskimo designs. But these were not nearly as efficient in holding body heat. Soon ready-made inexpensive European type clothing began to be worn, especially from spring through fall, but many Greenlanders still cling to two Eskimo designs. One is the skin boot, which is superior to anything the white man can provide that the Greenlander can afford, and the anorak. One sees anoraks everywhere, in every color, on every size male

Holiday costumes
showing the "pearl" collars and the long leather kamiks, *or boots.*

from toddlers taking their first steps to old men quietly sunning themselves as they puff away at their pipes. One more advantage of the anorak is that unlike white men's coats, which require collars and ties to make them look tidy and complete, the anorak provides all the costume necessary to make the upper part of a man's body look well dressed.

When traveling in summer along the coast, except for the national costume, one is not likely to see fur clothing until he is well north of the Arctic Circle. The fuzzy polar bear trousers that once marked the Greenland hunter are now seen only in the northernmost settlements. Holsteinsborg, a village near 67° North latitude is a likely place for the first pair of sealskin trousers to turn up. This is also the first settlement, coming from the South, where sled dogs are seen about town. In deference to the growing sheep industry in southern Greenland, sled dogs are forbidden by law south of Holsteinsborg. In any case, dogs were never as important in southern Greenland as in the North.

Two Greenland girls in modern dress.

TWO *The Saga Period, the Middle Ages and a Mystery*

Back in the year 981 when Erik the Red was outlawed from Iceland on a manslaughter charge, he decided to spend his three-year exile in finding the land that a man named Gunnbjorn had reported seeing around 900. He left Iceland with his wife and children, his slaves and their families, and possibly some neighbor families too. The party numbered twenty or thirty and carried aboard their ship as was customary in Viking times, cattle, sheep and dogs, perhaps also goats, pigs and poultry.

Erik returned to Iceland when his sentence was up and reported that not only had he found Gunnbjorn's land, but that he had explored it and found it fair. Believing that a pleasant name would attract more settlers, he named it Green Land, the saga tells. Erik's notion worked, for when he returned to colonize his Green Land in 985, twenty-five ships accompanied him. Some of these turned back, others were lost en route, but fourteen got through successfully. These Scandinavians were the nucleus of a colony that was to grow and thrive for centuries.

It was one of Erik's sons, Leif the Lucky, who, homeward bound for Green Land—or Greenland as it became later—

after a winter at the Norwegian court, missed his way and discovered the North American mainland. The Norwegian king, Olaf Tryggvason, whose hospitality he had enjoyed for a season, was an enthusiastic Christian, and had been converting heathen Norwegians in great numbers. Many felt, though, that the great number of conversions was directly related to the king's growing military strength. King Olaf forced some missionaries for converting the Greenlanders on the reluctant Leif, who knew his father would be little pleased. For Erik shared the belief with other full-blooded men of that time, that Christianity was an effeminate as well as an alien religion. True, there were already a few converts to the new religion in both Iceland and Greenland, but they were mainly women, slaves and men of low rank. It was unfashionable for men of high degree and proper spirit to embrace what was considered a weakly faith.

However in the year 1000, King Olaf sent messages to Iceland and Greenland stating his desire that they become Christian. His reputation for following up such "requests" with military expeditions was well known, and both countries hastily adopted the new religion. So Greenland became a Christian nation officially, probably at the next meeting of the *Althing*, as the national parliament was called, in 1001.

Greenland was colonized by Icelanders, so it was not surprising that they adopted the same form of government used in the country of their birth. We know that sometime after 1000 Greenland was a republic, resembling a New England town meeting, with an elaborate code of laws, and educated law speakers, or law men to pronounce it to the populace at the *Thing*. These were gatherings held both locally and nationally, when people with grievances met to present their cases, disputes were settled, punishments were meted out, and important announcements were made. The Thing also served the useful function of providing a time and place for visiting, for people would travel long distances to attend, and young people had a chance to meet one another. The republic flourished from about 990 to 1261, when the Greenlanders decided to join Norway. This is no mean record,

Statue of Leif Eriksson in Reykjavik, Iceland.

if we remember that it is almost a hundred years longer than the United States has thus far existed.

The men who came to Greenland with Erik, and those who followed to swell the Scandinavian population to an estimated 9,000, were by no means disappointed with the new country. They selected their farmsteads with care and it is a testimonial to their keen eyes and pastoral judgment that their cultivated hay fields are almost the only ones that are still being cultivated in Greenland today. One can actually see the dimensions of most of them, for the fertilizing done by the original colonists a thousand years ago produced thicker vegetation than the nearby unfertilized meadows. Though no actual fence outlines the boundaries, the taller, greener grass still marks the borders sharply enough to provide a little thrill of appreciation, remembering that the benefits provided by Vikings a thousand years ago are still being reaped today.

The great sport throughout Europe and much of the East during medieval times was hawking, or falconry. Kings set the fashion and noblemen and lesser lights followed their lead slavishly. Everybody knew about it, was interested in it and talked about it. Even a lowly farmer who might never own a hawk of his own was likely to know all about the superiority of one type over another and the tricks involved in training and handling them. Something like the way today's baseball fan, who does not play himself, will take pride in knowing the bat-

Greenland falcons.

ting averages or the pitching records of his favorite players.

In those days not only people but their hunting birds as well were classified according to rank. The golden eagle was considered the mightiest bird and was reserved for emperors and kings. The white Greenland falcon stood next in rank and was favored by royal princes. So popular was the sport that a special dispensation permitted even the clergy to take part. Mass might be celebrated in hunting costume, boots and spurs providing the clue to what lay beneath the priest's cassock, and falcons might perch on a corner of the altar during the service. If the celebrant was a Prince of the Church it would be a white Greenland or Iceland falcon that waited obediently for his master to finish his holy duties so they might both be off to the hunt.

As an illustration of how highly prized was the Greenland falcon and the huge distances that were traveled to secure them, the following segment of history is illuminating. Around 1394 during the Crusades, the Saracens captured a son of the Duke of Burgundy. As was customary, a ransom was set and, because his rank was high, so was the ransom. In this case it was twelve Greenland falcons. Since the birds were never raised in captivity, but always captured in the wild, a special expedition was probably made to Greenland to secure them. In any case, two years later the ransom was paid, the Duke's son released, and Saracen princes doubtless gloried in possessing the keen and fearless birds that had been born half a world away from their new homes, indeed beyond the Atlantic.

For complicated reasons, after Greenland elected to join Norway in 1261, the foreign ships that came to the northerly island became fewer and fewer until by the fifteenth century they had ceased entirely. The last undisputed Norwegian voyage took place in 1410, but relations with the Church authorities at the Vatican continued until past 1500. Contact with Iceland probably continued longest because of close blood ties and its geographical proximity. There were probably sporadic trading and whaling voyages following this period, but none entered the historical records. Except for a few short visits by Elizabethan explorers like Martin Frobisher, John Davis and Henry Hudson, no regular contact with the outside world was established again until the eighteenth century. The more than 200-year-long silence has provided us with a mystery that has tantalized scholars ever since.

One of the many clues that increases the mystery is that hooded cloaks found in Greenland's permafrost are of a fashion which started on the Continent around 1450, and which we think reached Greenland from England around 1480. This was after regular legal voyages from Norway had ceased. But apparently there were many illegal voyages which naturally enough never entered the historical records.

Following Erik the Red's time and throughout the Middle Ages, Greenlanders paid their church tithes to Rome in the form of live polar bears, live falcons, walrus ivory, and narwhal tusks, as well as milk products and animal hides. The sheep brought by the colonists throve, and Greenland proved an even better sheep country than Iceland. In our own century sheep raising has been revived and despite occasional harsh winters which create feeding difficulties, is doing well once more.

Since Greenland is a treeless country, the early colonists made voyages to Labrador, where they cut timber in quantity. When their own needs were satisfied, they used the surplus for trading with Iceland, which is also practically treeless. This timber was used for ship building, for house posts and rafters, and for utensils. Most Greenland buildings had walls of stone, for which we have reason to be grateful. Stone as a building material, with its lasting qualities, permits modern archaeologists to study almost every house, farm building and church from the early period. Thanks to the Icelandic sagas, and other records, we know the names of the men who originally dwelt at many of the steads; the size of the barns gives an idea of the number of their cattle and sheep. One of the farms uncovered by archaeologists has a stable with space for 104 cows. This would be a large dairy farm in modern Europe and not so small even in the United States.

Thanks to permafrost we even know how the colonists dressed, for some graves have yielded full costumes in which

Farming scenes in southwestern Greenland.

both the design and material are preserved. Hooded cloaks and other types of clothing worn by Greenlanders in the Middle Ages may be seen today in the wonderful Ethnographical Museum in Copenhagen. They are said to be the only examples of actual fifteenth century fashions which have survived to this day.

When the notion of re-introducing sheep into Greenland first arose, a scientific survey was made. The report was favorable and in 1915, 300 sheep were imported and placed in the southerly Julianehaab area for the purpose of providing initial stock for the Greenlanders who wanted to become full or part time sheep farmers. In 1953 the flocks had increased to 20,000, after the same number had been slaughtered for food. A government sheep breeding station studies the problems connected with the new industry and provides experts to train new herders and give advice to old.

The native caribou had been practically exterminated by overhunting when the government, looking for a food source to replace the dwindling supply of sea mammals, introduced 300 domestic reindeer from Norway into the Godthaab district in 1952. They are now doing well and the grazing in the Godthaab area near the government experimental farm seems ideal. When they were only a few months old, calves born in 1953 were as large as the biggest old females in the original shipment. A young Greenlander, sent to Finnmarken for several years where he was trained under experienced Lapp herders, is now in charge of the animals.

Besides sheep and reindeer the domestic animals in Greenland are negligible. The last census showed 20 goats, 60 head of cattle, 150 Icelandic ponies and between two and three thousand chickens.

Erik the Red, who explored most of the southwestern shore of Greenland, chose one of the most beautiful spots in all the land for his farm which he named Brattahlid, or Steep Mountain. Today this area is the Julianehaab District. Stone ruins of Erik's buildings as well as those of his fellow colonists are still visible, including Gardar, the residence of Greenland's earliest bishops. On the quiet shores of a long blue fjord, are the

A little Greenlander examining the saplings which were planted in an afforestation project.

towering mountains which inspired the naming of Erik's farm and the outlines of the farms cultivated a thousand years ago by the earliest Scandinavian settlers.

At Gardar in Igaliko the summers are especially warm, and while an Iowa farmer might not consider the soil ideal, it supports a healthy and prosperous family. The then Prime Minister of Denmark, Erik Eriksen, a visitor in 1953, was greeted there by a happy throng representing the best of the new Greenlanders. Songs and speeches by the villagers, bedecked in national costume, were followed by refreshments, slices of locally made cheese spread with fresh, sweet butter, and eaten with draughts of rich milk. As I was a member of the party I can say that, like the Prime Minister, I found it delicious.

To welcome the Prime Minister, arches had been erected, and then covered entirely with flowers. The sunshine was warm, the sky was clear and blue and as we approached the village on foot the magnificent, unaccompanied part singing, for which the Greenlanders are famous, greeted us softly and gradually grew louder. Here we saw for the first time numerous Icelandic ponies which are used for farm work as well as for getting about the roadless mountain terrain. The colorful scene provided by the villagers, the stunning background provided by Erik's mountains, the fine weather and the flawless singing, the feeling of having gone back a thousand years in history, conspired to make this one of the memorable moments in a summer crowded with new and lovely experiences.

Around the seventeenth century the Danes and Norwegians who then shared the same king, renewed their search for the Icelandic colonists in Greenland. A Norwegian missionary, Hans Egede, made the first permanent, modern settlement at Godthaab in 1721. He found the ruins of Norse homes, farms and churches, but no people he recognized as Scandinavian. Some scholars think now that the men and women he mistook for pure-blooded Eskimos, because they spoke only Eskimo and lived Eskimo fashion, were mixed blood descendants of the original colonists, who, when ships stopped coming from

Europe, adopted the Eskimo way of life in order to survive. Others think the Eskimos killed off the Scandinavians. Those who have most studied Eskimo ways are most opposed to this theory as being out of character; Fridtjof Nansen, a foremost historian as well as explorer and statesman, is one of these.

These Norse ruins formed the residence of the Bishop of Greenland in Viking times, a millennium ago.

THREE

Danish Policy and Modern Greenland

SHORTLY after the arrival of Hans Egede, Greenlanders began to learn to read and write. Each year the art spread, and when compulsory education was established, at the start of this century, it was not long before illiteracy was abolished throughout Greenland. The cultural level of the Greenlanders, even at its remote settlements, is far above anything known in northern Alaska or Canada. This was borne out strikingly when the Danish explorer Knud Rasmussen with his Greenlandic companions made a journey across Arctic America. Rasmussen, familiar with Danish policies which had improved the lot of the Eskimos in Greenland, was shocked to discover that comparatively nothing at all was done for the Eskimo in Canada and Alaska in the way of educational and health measures.

A major reason for this striking difference is that from earliest times Danish educators, instead of imposing a foreign language on their pupils, thus complicating further a difficult task, began by themselves learning the difficult Eskimo language. Soon they were able to teach the Greenlanders *in their own tongue.* All linguists agree that the Eskimo language is one of the most difficult in the world to learn. But instead of throwing up their hands and deciding it was impossible, as most Alaskan and Canadian teachers did, these missionary-schoolmasters set themselves patiently and painstakingly to learn. They made dictionaries, grammars, hymn books, in Eskimo. Most important, they taught the Greenlanders themselves to be teachers, clergymen, typesetters, illustrators, printers of books of their own composition in their own language. Thus the modern Greenlander already has a literary tradition. Local newspapers, many of them only mimeographed, but others well printed and illustrated, are published, and one *Atuagagdliutit* has been publishing without a break for almost a hundred years.

It is typical of Danish policy that instead of forcing Danish on the Greenlanders, it is only recently—and then in response to requests from the Greenlanders themselves—that classes are beginning to be *conducted* in Danish as well as Greenlandic. Today, in the larger settlements, parents may choose between two types of schooling for their children, with a Danish or a Greenlandic emphasis. High schools are using Danish more now. Talented pupils desiring education beyond what Greenland can offer are sent at government expense to Denmark to the universities and technical schools there. A real effort has long been made to train and hire natives for administrative positions wherever possible.

Eskimos in all countries are known for their mechanical skill and ingenuity. The story has now been told from almost every part of the Arctic of the native whose dollar watch finally stopped working, and who, though he had never done such a thing before, took it apart, cleaned it, made a new part to replace the worn one, and set it to running again. Special skills like these are being utilized in Greenland now, for instance at Holsteinsborg, where there is a shipbuilding and repairing yard. Four junior technical classes now turn out graduates ready to play useful roles in the many new local industries—at the shrimp canning factories, in the cod fishing industry, and so on. The equipment and training offered the boys at these schools is good, the standards of learning high.

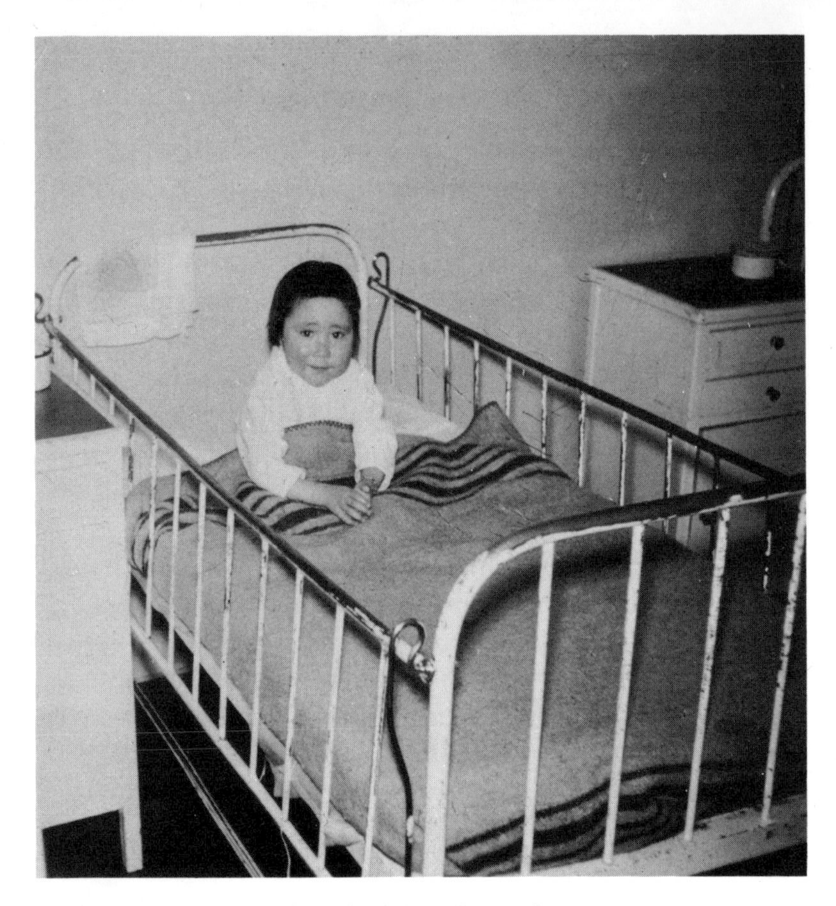

A little patient in a modern Greenland hospital.

Top men in each class are sent to Denmark for advanced training and all of the expenses are met by the government. Greenland has native radio operators, mechanics and skilled electrical workers. Nursing, teaching and midwifery are among the careers open to Greenland women which involve training in Denmark. Women have voting equality with the men, both in local and in national elections.

Greenlanders have developed an intense curiosity about the world outside. Their newspapers and magazines are crammed with articles on world affairs—debates at the United Nations, the activities of the Danish royal family, speeches and policies of the United States. Especially they like to hear about their own King and Queen. Like the majority of Danes, the King and his family may be observed riding their bicycles through Copenhagen streets as well as riding in state to formal affairs. This Greenland wants to see in still and moving pictures, especially since 1952 when the King and Queen visited Greenland and most of the population had a chance to observe first hand this charming, democratic pair.

Greenlanders have their special literary interests. They avidly read books by Knud Rasmussen, the famous Danish explorer who grew up in Greenland and was himself part Eskimo. Some of the great literary classics have been published in Greenland. Victor Hugo, and Alexander Dumas may be purchased, in Eskimo, at the local *boutik*, or general store, as well as lamps, woolens by the yard, imported foods and gadgets. Each store has, in Eskimo and Danish, a book section offering poetry, fiction, non-fiction in addition to innumerable "how-to" books—all in Eskimo.

What of the interest of the outside world in Greenland? It lies mainly in three fields. First is scientific: one has only to visit any large library and examine a single series of books "Information about Greenland," which now numbers more than 150 volumes, all devoted to some aspect of Greenland, to realize that the entire country has been a scientific laboratory for a long time.

Years before I ever set foot in Greenland my imagination had been completely captured by the little scientific station at Godhavn, in northern Greenland, that Morten Porsild, the Danish botanist, had founded and maintained alone for so many years. There was something appealing and admirable about a scientist who had the vision of a permanent house of arctic science to be built on the beautiful shores of Disko Island. A place where he and others like him could work in comfort on long term investigations. I had gathered every available scrap of published material about the area, about Porsild and the station itself. I talked with people who knew or had visited him during his many working years north of the Circle. Through his son Erling, who also chose botany for his profession, I had obtained photographs and much information. One picture in particular had been stamped with indelible ink on my mind, that of a kindly, bearded, anorak-coated scientist gazing calmly out of his many-paned study window at a procession of stunning icebergs moving slowly past.

In 1953 when my husband and I were invited by the Danish Government to be their guests on an extensive Greenland tour, one of the spots that I looked forward to seeing with quickened heartbeat was the station at Godhavn, the capital of north Greenland. Fortune favored us for we arrived there on a gorgeous sunny day in late July. The sky was blue, the grass was green and the red and white Danish flags were snapping smartly in the breeze at the landing stage, newly erected the year before in honor of the royal visit. It happened to be my birthday and our mood was gay.

We entered the station. With an involuntary cry of recognition I ran to "Porsild's window" and there, miraculously, was the iceberg parade. A new generation of bergs to be sure, but sufficiently like the originals to which I had devoted a chapter in my book *Within the Circle* to give me the eerie feeling that "I had been there before."

Farther on in the station, which still houses a director, visiting scientist and a fine library, although Porsild has gone, a secretly prepared, truly Greenlandic feast awaited us. Innumerable tiny, sweet shrimps from the rich Disko Bay shrimp beds, local fish delicatedly prepared, reindeer meat, and local berries. Even the beer, an absolute necessity among Danes for ceremonial toasting purposes, was Greenlandic. Dr. Paul Gelting the scientist in charge of the station told us proudly that he had brewed it himself. The fairy-tale quality of a dream come true persisted through the day. It was much the nicest birthday party I ever had.

One of the dividends resulting from the exploration by scientists has been the discovery and then the utilization of mineral resources. Cryolite is a rare and valuable mineral used in the aluminum industry. It is found in its natural form in Greenland in sufficient quantity to justify the long voyages it must make to reach manufacturing centers. About a century ago, mining operations were started at Ivigtut, on the west coast. Here a huge open pit mine provides ore, one third of which comes to the United States, the rest going to Copenhagen and thence to the rest of Europe. Ivigtut is one of only two highly industrialized spots in all Greenland, and the only one on the west coast.

The other is Mesters Vig on the east coast, far north of the Circle at 72° North latitude. It was here that Lauge Koch on one of his annual expeditions to East Greenland reported the existence of lead and zinc in 1948. This led to the building of a brand new modern village numbering about 1,000 by the summer of 1955 on the virtually uninhabited east coast of the island. Recently lead mining operations began and in mid-summer of 1956 the first shipments started on their way outside. Power

The open-pit cryolite mine at Ivigtut. Cryolite is a very lightweight, white mineral used in the manufacture of aluminum.

station, laboratory, hospital and engineering shops have been constructed as well as an eight-mile road over the permafrost from King Oscars Fjord to the mine. Six miles from the village an air strip keeps Mesters Vig in touch with the outside world, supplying mail, provisions, personnel and spare parts for machinery. Without air communication, the engineers, geologists and miners who make up the population, would be cut off from the rest of the world for more than ten months of the year, starting in September. During the short summer all the material mined throughout the year must be shipped out with the help of specially built ice-breaking vessels.

Coal is found in many parts of Greenland, but the only deposits so far discovered are of a poor quality, with only about half the heat strength of ordinary commercial coal. No attempt is made to produce more than enough for home use. Disko Island has the main coal mine, but investigations continue in hope of finding a better quality coal. Greenland must still import about 8,000 tons a year. Formerly she supplied all her own fuel needs; but since the war, industry though still small, has been stepped up, and the new housing program has also increased the demand for the fuel.

There are some who deplore the building of modern Danish style homes which require costly coal for heating, and imported lumber to build, remembering the Eskimo style house of sod which cost nothing but labor and was so well designed against cold that the heat from blubber lamps used to cook meals was enough to keep it cozy.

Peter Freuchen who built the first European style house at Thule and gave it its name, begins his autobiographical *Vagrant Viking* with these poignant lines:

"The Eskimos are moving away from Thule these days. They are deserting their ancient settlement. I read in the papers that two spokesmen for the Thule Eskimos have gone to Copenhagen to ask the Danish Government to move their village to the north, away from the deafening noise of the American airplanes . . . modern civilization has moved in and Thule . . . has been turned into one of the world's major airports."

Present-day buildings at Thule.

The spokesmen for the Thule Eskimos were successful in Copenhagen and the entire village was moved about ninety miles northward to a site named Kranak where the shrieking jet planes could no longer be heard. Freuchen says "polar bears no longer come to Pitufik across the bay from Thule; instead there are seven thousand soldiers." Those Europeans who knew Greenland in the old days mourn the exchange, as do the older Greenlanders who recall the satisfactory pleasures of the days when a man needed no money to be healthy, successful, happy and respected.

But the younger Greenlanders are not mourning. They are far too busy learning Danish and other languages, and a trade, and they hope to travel to Denmark and farther. They are working for more modern schools for their children, for an end to the tuberculosis scourge, modern housing and sanitation, and toward the feeling that they are no longer an isolated people, but citizens of the world.

III

Iceland:

THE MOST LITERATE LAND IN THE WORLD

White River Lake, and a glacier, in Iceland.

ONE

Frost, Fire and Geysers

IMAGINE one of the most volcanic areas in the world; set down beside it one of the most active glacial regions; surround it with lush green farms nestling at the feet of steep-sided, treeless fjords; bathe it in the clearest imaginable atmosphere. Then people it with an ancient folk, tall and handsome, who care more for poetry, art, chess and history than for wealth, and a picture of "little" Iceland begins to emerge. This mountainous isle, which rises from the Gulf Stream waters of the North Atlantic between Greenland and Europe, has been rightly called the Land of Frost and Fire.

Visitors asked to choose the single most interesting thing about Iceland would seldom agree. Animal lovers would be sure to select the Iceland pony, a unique and charming breed, larger than a Shetland but smaller than the usual horse, with thick long mane and tail. Sports fishermen would praise the salmon streams to which they make pilgrimages from Europe and the United States. Literary people would nominate the famous Icelandic sagas, though a few specialists might pick her Viking Age court poets who recited before kings in many a European state. Students of democracy would agree on her parliament, established in 930 A.D. which earned her, long before England, the title of Mother of Parliaments. Romantics might choose piracy, the country's chief industry for centuries. Chess enthusiasts would remember that Iceland has produced famous players for eight or nine hundred years and scholars have written whole books devoted to the subject, like Willard Fiske's *Chess in Iceland.*

Thanks to the country's extraordinary physical features, geologists have called it the most interesting natural laboratory in the world. Artists, both native and foreign, have praised and painted its strange beauty and debated the causes of the incredible clarity of the island's atmosphere. But to an outsider with no special interest, by far the most interesting single thing Iceland has ever produced is her people.

To better appreciate the striking qualities of an Icelander, a few geographical facts are needed. Iceland is closer to Greenland than to any other large land; only 180 miles separates them. Norway, the nearest European mainland country, is 645 miles to the east; Scotland, a like distance to the southeast. Northeasternmost Greenland actually extends farther eastward than any part of Iceland, which definitely captures Iceland for the Western Hemisphere, geographically. Whatever the geographers decide, however, the Icelanders prefer to think of themselves as Europeans, since they say it was there that they and their language and culture originated.

Thule, as Iceland was known to the Greeks and to the Latins down to Columbus, is 40,000 square miles, a fifth larger than Ireland, a fifth smaller than Pennsylvania. But four-fifths of it, the central portion, is an uninhabitable desert. Volcanic eruptions have left huge lava flats in their wake, and more than twenty volcanoes have erupted in historic times.

Mt. Hekla, one of the most active, was thought during the Middle Ages to be one of the two entrances of hell (the other, in Sicily, was Etna). Those who saw Hekla's last eruption in 1946, when red-hot lava spilled from her cone down the mountainside, might be inclined to agree on the gate-of-hell matter. Another folk tale was that Iceland was inhabited by giants who attacked sailors and ships by hurling hot rocks at any who dared approach their shores. It is easy to imagine that the tale was born when some ancient sailors, approaching Iceland during a volcanic eruption, met a thunderous rain of exploding rocks.

Iceland's history is marked by many disastrous volcanic explosions, each a courier of bad news to follow. First came the molten lava which destroyed everything in its path. Then the rains of volcanic ash followed and darkened everything locally for many days. Some drifted halfway round the world to darken the skies of people who never heard of Iceland. As the ash settled on farm meadows it killed the vegetation. Without grass the livestock starved; without livestock the people starved. This was the cue for disease to enter the picture, to decimate the population and complete the tragic cycle.

Lava deserts produced by the terrible and mysterious workings of the earth's interior cover large portions of Iceland. They are flanked by another kind of desert produced by opposite conditions. This is the ice desert, more than thirty permanent ice fields. This spreads over one-eighth of the country. Five of these glaciers are larger than twenty-five square miles in area, and one, Vatnajökull, is larger than any in Europe. It is here, in glacial fields, that all of Iceland's main rivers have their sources. As the glacial torrents rush down the mountains, they produce some of the most magnificent waterfalls in the world. These rapids and waterfalls combine with the numerous braided streams in the lowlands to make the rivers unnavigable. But there is a silver lining in the huge water power potential of these same rushing rivers with their falls.

Although Iceland, like Greenland, is virtually a treeless country, this was not true in the past. Birch forests covered much of the lowland when the first colonists arrived, but they were recklessly used for fuel and as charcoal in the making of weapons for the piracy industry, the famous Viking voyages. Extensive sheep grazing was effective in preventing new growth. Even then, Iceland never produced the tall straight timbers needed for ships' masts, or the thick houseposts every Norseman considered a semi-religious necessity for his dwelling place.

ABOVE *Mt. Hekla in eruption.* BELOW *Lava rock formations.*

ABOVE *One of the largest glaciers in Iceland.* BELOW *A waterfall produced by the glacial torrents rushing down the mountains.*

These were imported from Norway and from Labrador where the Greenlanders, between the eleventh and fourteenth centuries, used to secure both housebuilding and shipbuilding timber, some of which they traded to Iceland.

Today on the east coast of Iceland, at Hallormstadir, the Icelanders are experimenting with imported Sitka and Norwegian spruce and larch, and an extensive reforestation project is under way with heavy government support. Similar work is being done in many other places, particularly on the north coast, which has proved more favorable than the south coast for trees. It is hoped before many generations have passed that it will no longer be possible to refer to Iceland as a "treeless" country.

The ingenuity of the Icelander is beautifully displayed in the way he has turned what might seem a handicap into an asset. Thanks to being so volcanic, Iceland has thousands of hot springs. They occur usually in the fissures of the earth's crust, those giant wounds left behind by earthquake or volcano. There are many kinds of springs. Clear water springs, mineral water springs, sulphur springs, and some that are cauldrons of boiling mud. Some stand alone, sending tall wisps of steam aloft, others form clusters or single files along a valley floor, a characteristic Icelandic scene. As early as the thirteenth century the famous Icelandic historian Snorri Sturluson piped water from a hot spring to a bathing pool near his house [I have a picture of this bathing pool which is still in existence]. One never has to travel far in Iceland to get free hot water for bath or laundry.

Today these burbling, gushing hot springs have been harnessed and put to work. Reykjavik, Iceland's capital, derives its name, which means bay of smokes, or smoky bay, from the hot springs in the area which send wisps of steam resembling smoke into the air on a cold day. It is appropriate that Smoky Bay, which houses more than one third of the country's population, should heat its homes with volcanic hot water. Just below the boiling point, the naturally heated water is piped ten miles into the city. A municipal project makes it available, and every home owner simply pays a moderate fee and hooks on to the main line. The system was completed soon after World War II and keeps the modern houses warm and cozy on the most bone-chilling windy days. No ashes need to be carried out; the heating bill is a fraction of what it used to be when coal had to be imported; and, best of all, the city is now free of coal dust and smog. Reykjavik is one of those spotless, shining Scandinavian cities in which all take pride.

One of the greatest surprises awaiting visitors to Iceland is her climate. Probably because of her name, most people expect it to be cold, but Iceland has what is known as an oceanic climate, which never gets very warm in summer and never very cold in winter. The air which arrives in Iceland has traveled long distances over a warm sea, acquiring both heat and moisture, which it presents in the form of higher winter

A pumping station for the natural (volcanic) hot water used to heat the homes in Reykjavik, Iceland.

temperatures, and either as rain or as snow which stays days or weeks, seldom for months except in the North or on mountains. The Gulf Stream warms the waters bathing Iceland's shores, but its outer edge produces fog by brushing shoulders with colder currents. The polar waters sometime touch the northern and western coasts of the island and have a chilling effect on local temperatures.

Sea ice is rarely visible from any coast of Iceland from September through December. It is rare at any time on the southern parts of both east and west coasts; it has never been seen on the south coast, unless just at Iceland's southwest corner. Toward the end of winter and early spring, pack ice from the North may actually touch the northwestern coast and has been known to pile up on the shores and block the harbors.

A peculiarity of Iceland's weather is that the same kind seldom prevails throughout the country. When it is cloudy in the South, it is usually clear in the North and vice versa. This is useful knowledge for airplane pilots who can land at Akureyri in the North if Keflavik is closed in. The famous Iceland fog, frequent in the East, is less so in the North and almost entirely absent in the South and West. As in other northern lands, thunderstorms are rare.

Evidence that Reykjavik, on the southwestern coast of Iceland, does not have severe winters is that the pond in the middle of the city seldom freezes long enough for the children to learn to skate. January is the coldest month and its average mean temperature is 33° above zero, Fahrenheit, or almost two degrees warmer than New York City. The January temperature is similar to that of Milan, Italy, or Philadelphia, Pennsylvania. Temperatures seldom rise above 70°, Fahrenheit, in summer, and while it may be rainy and windy in winter, the thermometer seldom goes lower than freezing.

Volcanic heat is used to good purpose in large hothouses where since 1935 vegetables and flowers have been raised commercially. Without a cheap source of heat the cost would be prohibitive.

Icelandic law requires every child graduating from elementary school to be able to swim. It is volcanic heat that warms the swimming pool that is standard equipment in every school in the country. Farmers as well as city people use the local hot springs, and it is a familiar sight to see vapor puffing toward the sky in a lone farmyard.

The earliest Icelanders, variously known as Vikings, Norsemen or Northmen, really just Scandinavians, were notoriously brave. One might even say that physical courage was a part of their religion. But they possessed no scientific explanations for the unique physical features of the country and resorted to magical reasoning to explain them. How often they must have alternated between fear and wonder as hot springs suddenly shot streams of boiling water into the sky, or volcanoes spewed forth molten rock in all directions to the accompaniment of ear shattering explosions, smoke, steam and ash.

Perhaps most awful of the extraordinary Icelandic natural wonders is the phenomenon with the jaw-breaking name of *jökullhlaup*, which means glacier (jökull) burst (hlaup). This occurs when a hot spring is located beneath a glacier. It melts the surrounding glacier, creating an under-ice lake which has no place to go. Eventually pressure is created, usually with the help of volcanic activity, to explode or burst the glacier. Now, instead of molten lava erupting, it is ice and water that rush out at unimaginable speed to ravage the nearest valley. Ice chunks, as large as cathedrals, as well as smaller bits, are hurtled down slopes, wiping out everything in their path—people, buildings, animals. Usually there is little warning before the onset of a jökullhlaup, but certain glaciers are known to have hot springs beneath them and to break out periodically. Survivors of one burst may leave before the next, but a surprising number stay behind, rebuild and reoccupy their farms, despite the future's threat.

TWO

Viking Times

WHEN the Scandinavians "discovered" Iceland around 850 A.D., they found Irish people there whose leaders had sought and found in Thule an ideal spot for solitary religious contemplation, a popular way of life among ninth-century Irish. With the arrival of numerous Vikings, who were the best known and most feared desperadoes of their time, many of the Irish fled. But in one sense the Irish survived in Iceland.

While most Icelanders consider their blood to be largely Norwegian, the next largest component is Irish. Indeed, according to the scientists who depend largely on blood type and other physical tests, the Irish part may be as much as sixty per cent of the whole.

The first part of the mixing came about through the Norwegians having conquered a large part of Ireland, following the year 800, and then being crowded out by the Irish after two or three generations, when many of them sailed for Iceland with their blended families and apparently with a good many Irish friends who decided to come along.

Then developed Icelandic buccaneering, mixed trading and piracy voyages, which reached as far south as the Mediterranean coast of Africa, with winterings sometimes as far east as

Constantinople. On the way home, whether the cruise had been only a part of a summer or for seasons, the returning buccaneers would go ashore on some coast, frequently Irish, and take a farm with all its people, beasts, goods, building timbers and even the hay, and off they went with the loot to Iceland. Northwestern Europe had slavery at this time and the slaves were seldom black. Those in Iceland were usually Irish, but there were German, Scottish and English slaves. Seldom did a Scandinavian make slaves of other Scandinavians, but one of them might rob another of his slaves.

Slavery wore itself out in Iceland after the first hundred years. Then came centuries of commerce in which Irish traders arrived with cargoes, sold them, perhaps for land, and did not return to Ireland.

Once the slaves were freed, and they often were after a few years had elapsed, they became regular citizens and intermarried freely with the Scandinavians. But the Norse were the aristocrats, and since the early records were largely family histories, it was the Norwegians who were mentioned most often in these sources. These two people form the main groups from which all Icelanders are descended. Danes, Swedes and all other Europeans made up perhaps ten per cent of the population. Sixty years after the start of the Norse colonization, there were 50,000 people in Iceland. Almost every farm occupied today was settled during this early period, and the Icelanders, who are great record keepers, can tell you the name of the first settlers and the names of the families who have occupied it ever since.

One man, a powerful king, was unintentionally responsible for the colonization of Iceland. The tyrannical Harald the Fairhaired was busy "uniting" all of Norway for the first time in its history by means of war or the threat of war. Every lesser king and chief in the land had to submit to his greater power, not easy in an age which glorified courageous *individual* action. Many of the chiefs, or Jarls (earls) as they were called, preferred to leave Norway rather than knuckle under to the powerful Harald. Some went to Scotland, Ireland and the Hebrides; the majority

Two Icelandic women in national costume at a state banquet.

went directly, or eventually, to Iceland. So the country was settled by Jarls and other nobility whose rank depended on their ancestors having been successful fighters, able organizers and wise administrators. Had they not possessed these virtues they would have been unable to maintain their positions. Naturally they were the kind of men who preferred being their own masters; they were leaders, willing to take a chance in a strange and difficult land. As Ellsworth Huntington has put it, it was the best of the best who founded Iceland. These rather special men and their families were thus able to create an almost unique community with a cultural level far above the average. They were to produce a literature seldom if ever matched in a country of such small numbers.

Iceland, which has been called the first American republic, once more became a democratic republic in entire control of her own affairs on June 17, 1944. The Icelandic Parliament, or Althing, the oldest surviving legislative assembly in Europe, was first established in 930 A.D. When Iceland joined Norway in 1262, thinking she was entering an equal partnership, she discovered that the canny Norwegians thought and acted differently, and the power of the Althing began to decline. The decline continued after 1380 when Iceland came under the Danish crown, which ruled for the next 500 years. In 1800 the Althing was abolished except that its upper house still retained its judicial functions, resembling those of the British House of Lords. Forty-three years later it was revived and slowly grew again in power. What might be called a dominion status was yielded by the Danes to Iceland in 1874 at the millennial celebration of its colonization in 874. Full Parliamentary government returned in 1904, although Denmark continued to control Iceland's relations with the outside world until 1918. In that year she became entirely independent, but agreed to share the same king with the Danes for a twenty-five-year period. In 1944 a plebicite was held and Icelanders voted almost unanimously to become a republic.

Iceland now has a president, elected every four years. His duties and powers are more like those of France than of the United States. So Iceland's president has many of the prerogatives and functions of the king of a limited monarchy. The present (1956) leader of the country, who resides at beautiful Bessastadir, Iceland's White House, is Asgeir Asgeirsson, elected in 1952, who is a former Prime Minister, member of parliament, bank director and educator.

Iceland may no longer have a king, but in one sense at least every Icelander is a king. For just as people refer to their royalty and nobility by first names, King John or Prince Henry, so do Icelanders refer to each other. There are no family names. Icelandic telephone books list a man's first name followed by his father's name. Johann Bjornsson is listed under the J's, the Bjornsson (son of Bjorn) simply indicates his father's name. Johann's son will be Vilhjalmur Johansson and so on. This is the way it has always been in Iceland, and to preserve the old

Icelandic children.

order a law has forbidden the use of family names, except for a few that existed at the time the law was passed.

You might think this would make it difficult, if not impossible, to keep track of a family's history, but not for an Icelander. He is passionately fond of geneology and not only is he able to trace his own ancestry back to the settlement of Iceland or earlier, but he is more than likely to know the family trees of many of his relatives, friends and neighbors, and precisely how they are related to each other. The Icelander lavishes as much effort and enthusiasm on geneology as we do on baseball. Both my husband's parents were Icelandic, and he is able to trace his ancestry back to the first white child born on the North American mainland during Thorfinn Karlsefni's unsuccessful colonizing expedition in 1003 A.D.

Incidentally, a woman keeps her same name throughout life whether or not she marries. She never takes her husband's name, except perhaps when traveling abroad in order to avoid endless discussions with hotel room clerks. If her name is Helga Arngrimsdottir (Arngrim's daughter) it remains that—she never becomes Mrs. anyone. Long before women in the United States or Britain were granted a voice in their own government, Icelandic women had won the right to vote. They began voting in local elections as early as 1882 and in general elections in 1915. Nearly all positions are now open to women as well as men.

An Icelandic housewife sitting by her well-filled bookshelves.

THREE

The Literary Heritage

A THOUSAND years ago everyone throughout Scandinavia spoke the same language. No marked regional differences then separated Norwegian speech from that of the Swede, Dane or Icelander, though they do now. In the millennium that followed, neighboring idioms and bits of language invaded all Scandinavian borders except Iceland's, blending, flavoring and changing the local speech. Partly because Iceland lay isolated far out in the ocean, and long sea voyages rather than short overland journeys were required for visiting foreign shores, the language changed little. A literary tongue changes less than those merely spoken; Icelandic was kept from rapid alteration by its Eddas, sagas and scaldic poetry as English has been constrained in recent centuries by Shakespeare and the King James version of the Bible. Changes have been so few that today any school child able to read can understand and enjoy the sagas.

The sagas form a great prose library dealing with the history and legend of the Scandinavian countries chiefly, but also with other countries from Russia to Turkey. Some of them have purely Icelandic backgrounds and are essentially family histories. Most of them were composed in the ninth, tenth and eleventh centuries, when they were memorized, recited aloud and passed on intact from one generation to the next.

They were not written down until the end of the thirteenth century, and then there occurred a most important and fortunate event. Throughout Europe at the time Latin alone was considered a suitable tongue for scholars and scholarship, though it was known by only a fraction of the population. But instead of being recorded in Latin, as would have happened elsewhere, they were penned in the Icelandic vernacular—the everyday language understood by all. And rather than a mere handful of clerics knowing this glorious literature, master and servant alike enjoyed the tales during long winter evenings when all would gather in the largest room in the house to listen. During the recital, women would mend, knit and sew; men would carve wood, card wool or repair their tools quietly. So it happened that the brave deeds, the wise, witty and noble sayings, and the grand ideals of their ancestors became familiar to *all* the Icelanders, who loved them and made them a part of their everyday culture. They have remained so.

Helgi Briem tells us that "when the reader paused, the audience discussed the people described, and lauded or censured their acts, thus forming the character and opinion of the younger people, giving them a feeling of their common heritage." The sagas were first written on parchment, some of them hundreds of pages long. They were lovingly and painstakingly copied, many were exquisitely illustrated and illuminated, and the art of both reading and writing spread quickly throughout the country.

Long before there were any formal schools, mothers and fathers taught their children to read and write, a tradition that continued for centuries and made possible Iceland's proud claim that, except for defectives, there has never been *any* illiteracy in the country.

While the sagas were essentially family histories, in telling about a man and his deeds, much of the larger history, of the customs, and a good deal of the flavor of life in Viking times was also communicated. The sagas number about forty, although there are many short stories besides. Some are known to be factual, for they dovetail and are confirmed by historical evidence; others are known to be just good stories, the fiction of their day. They also vary in quality, ranging from merely entertaining to world famous, acknowledged masterpieces. Probably their most widely recognized importance is that they preserved certain parts of European history, legend and lore that were wiped out elsewhere. As the Christian church moved northward into Europe, introducing the new religion, it was thought necessary to wipe out all knowledge of the old, heretical beliefs. Except in Iceland. Here it was the clergy themselves who were responsible for preserving the ancient knowledge, even if it was about heathen gods.

National Museum and Theater in Reykjavik.

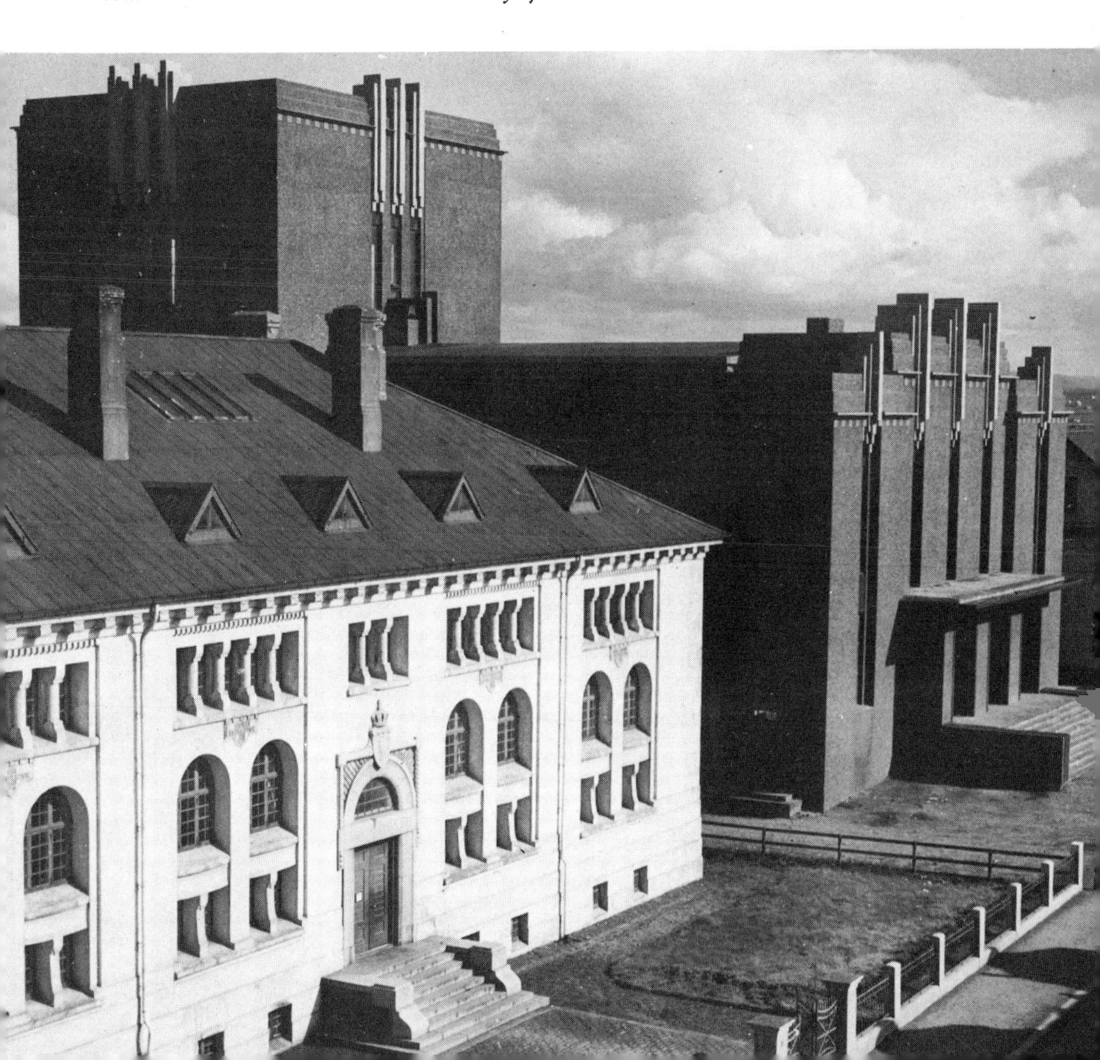

The rich and varied Icelandic literary heritage also includes the two monumental Eddas, which reach back to the earliest periods and were composed in both prose and verse. The Edda of Saemund the Wise, called the older, is known as the poetic Edda; the Edda of Snorri Sturluson, named the younger, is the prose Edda. Both are "calculated to inspire profound admiration for the character, valor and virtues" of the early Icelanders.

Love of the art of public speaking—the everyday custom of improvising poetry and prose which was recited and repeated to groups ranging from a handful of family to outdoor gatherings of thousands—fostered the literary surge which flowered during and after the time Iceland was settled. It coincided with the crest of energy and power that launched the bold Viking wave which penetrated throughout Europe, reaching Africa, Asia and America.

The form of writing used during the earliest period was runic. This alphabet is made from straight lines suitable for cutting in wood or stone. It was not a swift method of writing and was better for short, terse messages inscribed on memorial stones than for communicating poetry or history. The clergy brought in Latin script, in which the Eddas and sagas were preserved. Printing entered Iceland in 1525 or 1526. While the Bible and hymn books were first to be published, the Eddas and sagas soon followed.

The *rimur,* or narrative rhyme, period followed close on the heels of the saga age. During winter evenings, when the sun barely rose above the horizon, families continued to gather and take turns reading and reciting. Now the saga "readings" alternated with the chanting of the rimur.

The extremely complicated form of the rimur is nearly impossible to reproduce in English. Vilhjalmur Stefansson, equally fluent in Icelandic and English, published in 1904 some nonsense verse that closely approximates the complicated forms. Notice the inner rhymes in the following stanza as well as the usual ones at the end of the line. The alliteration, which plays an important role, contributes much to the crisp, musical result.

Andy *found* the flute had *sounded*
False, and *ground* his teeth in rage,
While the *hound,* with hope *unbounded*
Hopped *around* the barren stage.

In these days of radio, TV and other "ready-made" pleasures, it is hard to imagine a people so talented and trained that they could compose poems on the spur of the moment in such complicated forms. Apparently Icelanders have always been able to do it. They have had sufficient imagination to invent more than 2,000 separate forms of rimur alone, some of which read backwards and forwards with equal ease without disturbing the message. When you read others backwards you get a rebuttal of what the forward reading says.

Icelandic poetry has been written about every imaginable subject, but first place is reserved for the stirring, almost mystical love every Icelander feels for the beauties of the northern landscape. Even ponies have a large body of literature dedicated to them and "many an Icelandic steed has therefore had a funeral poem which a prince might envy."

As late as 1949, when my husband and I visited this literary land, all Icelanders knew the sagas and many could recite thousands of rimur. It was still customary to commemorate occasions by writing poems for them. Two such were written and read by their authors at the huge formal dinner given us by the Icelandic government. Folk songs with words supplied by Iceland's greatest poets were sung between courses. After numerous speeches, toasts and acknowledgments, the floor was cleared, and the evening brought to a close by dancing in which young and old alike took part, for the Icelanders are energetic as well as poetic.

Proof that tradition still flourishes is found in that Iceland publishes several times more books per capita than any other country in the world. Reykjavik alone supports twenty bookstores! A city of like size in the United States might have one, or at most two or three.

Since 1949, we are told, older people shake their heads and

complain that because of radio young people no longer take the interest their fathers did in literary matters. But new editions of the sagas do continue to be best sellers, despite their high cost. It is even conceivable that a radio voice will replace the person who read aloud during the winter evenings and may even be the means of upholding the literary tradition that some think is dying.

FOUR Iceland Since the War

ONE reason modern Iceland finds it easy to maintain and develop her scholarly reputation may be found in her far-above-the-average educational system. You don't need to be rich to go to any school in Iceland. All schooling is free, including attendance at the modern university, and postgraduate work abroad. In 1953, 759 students were attending the University of Reykjavik and 400 more were getting specialized training abroad, which makes one in every 150 Icelanders a college graduate, or better.

Besides the usual types, Iceland has many special technical schools. They cover naval training, arts and crafts, wireless and machine shop techniques, and commercial subjects. There are also teachers' training schools and those that specialize in domestic science and physical culture.

It is not uncommon in Iceland to meet a medical doctor who took a year's training at the Mayo Clinic in Minnesota, a geologist who earned his Ph.D. at Cornell, an engineer who is a graduate of M.I.T. In the past, Icelandic students went mainly to Scandinavia, England, Germany and Switzerland for their final studies. During World War II, when many of these places were cut off, they came in large numbers to North American universities, and have continued to do so ever since.

In addition to educating her citizens, Iceland feels she must encourage the creative arts. She does so by granting specially talented painters, sculptors and writers a stipend which permits them to continue their studies or work instead of having to shift to other jobs to support themselves. In 1955, 133 such grants were made in varying amounts. Iceland's most famous sculptor, the recently deceased Einar Jonsson, worked most of his life with a government subsidy which freed him from the necessity of making his art pay. It does not seem to have inhibited his output, for his sculpture now fills an entire museum.

All the Icelanders I have ever met are interested in art. I never entered an Icelandic home that did not have some original art work in it, whether it belonged to a fisherman or a prime minister. The paintings, of course, ranged in size from miniatures to huge oils covering an entire wall. It is easier for a painter to earn a living in Iceland than most other countries. It is common for all paintings at an exhibition in Reykjavik to be sold before the close of the show. Original paintings are also a traditional wedding present, so that there is a steady demand. Gudmundar Einarsson, one of the country's most talented painters, who is also a first-rate sculptor, writer and geologist, started the first ceramics works in Reykjavik. These have developed an international reputation, attracting many students from foreign countries.

Another form of art in which Icelanders show their taste and originality is in their architecture. It is surprising therefore to discover how few old buildings exist in Iceland, since they care deeply about their past and tend to preserve any evidences of it. The answer to the riddle is found in the building material used in old days. Houses used to be built of sod and wood, a most effective and inexpensive way of protecting one's self from the elements. But unlike stone, which lasts almost indefinitely, sod houses deteriorate quickly and new homes were built as needed. Abandoned houses eventually became part of the earth itself, leaving no bits and traces for archaeologists to discover in later

ABOVE *Sod houses in Iceland.* BELOW *In his homespun shirt, this farmer in Grimsey, Iceland, stands by the grass-grown turf wall of the "skemma," or storehouse.*

years. In the country one still sees farm buildings of sod, with grass growing thick and green on their roofs. But all new building is required by law to be of reinforced concrete. This is considered the safest form of construction for an earthquake-ridden country that remains one of the most volcanic in the world. Iceland's frequent earthquakes are indeed likeliest as the chief explanation of why houses are not built of stone. When the earth shakes, stone walls crumble and cause death.

All the new buildings are modern. Apartment houses and private homes both feature large picture windows to make the most of what sunny days come along. Even farmhouses follow the modern style. The government supplies free building plans to both city and country dweller if they want to build and need to save the cost of hiring a private architect. Those with the means and desire do, of course, hire their own architects and build more elaborate and unusual structures.

Building costs are high, so are rents, and there has been a housing shortage since World War II. To encourage new building, the government offers free plots of land outside Reykjavik for those who want to own their own homes. Nissen and Quonset huts made their appearance all over Iceland during the war, to provide shelter for the thousands of troops, first British and later American. After the war's end, the huts were bought by the Icelanders, painted bright colors, and are now to be seen mostly in the country, where they generally house farm machinery.

There are no railroads in Iceland. Feet and ponies provided the means for getting from one place to another in the early days. The charming, stocky little Iceland horses have great endurance and were used to ride from town to town and cross-country, as well as for farming. With the advent of roads, jeep, bus and plane, the sight of these handsome creatures, their thick manes and tails blowing like banners in the wind, is not nearly as common as it used to be. They now number only about 42,000. Still used for pleasure and sport, they are no longer raised in large numbers for export as formerly, when they were used extensively in British coal mines, till electricity took over.

ABOVE *A view of Akureyri, the second largest city in Iceland. In the distance is a modern church.* BELOW *A typical modern, reinforced concrete house in Reykjavik, Iceland.*

Iceland has comparatively few good through roads crossing the interior of the country. Reykjavik and Akureyri, the second largest city which lies in Eyjafjordur on the north coast, are connected by road. Like most railroadless countries, Iceland proved eager for aviation. The Icelanders fly regularly and often within their country and have an excellent overseas airline system. Ships retain their importance in the fishing industry and in the Atlantic passenger service, and cargo fleets are maintained, wholly and partly government owned. Coastal freight and summer pleasure cruise ships continue to ply the waters around Iceland, but to get from one town to another the Icelanders commonly fly.

Fishing is one of the main industries in Iceland, and accounts for the country's most important export.

The author and her husband, Vilhjalmur Stefansson, in Iceland.

As transatlantic flying developed, it became apparent that Iceland's geographical position gave her a new and special importance. She constitutes an ideal way station between North America and Europe, and the lessons of war strengthened our belief in her strategic military importance in guarding all shipping lanes in the North Atlantic.

Animal husbandry was once the chief occupation of the country, but today only thirty per cent of the Icelanders are so engaged. Sheep farming has always been the mainstay of the rural farmer, but in recent years sheep diseases have played havoc with the flocks. There are now about 400,000 sheep in the land, which is only half the number that once sought forage and

An Icelandic pony.

ran untended in Iceland's mountains in summertime. Sheep roundups are held in the fall when each farmer pulls his own animals from the flock by finding his own mark which is cut in the ear of the sheep when they are young. Cattle are of relatively minor importance in Iceland; there are only about 45,000 in the entire country.

Grass is the chief crop in Iceland. Oats and barley are beginning to be cultivated in some parts of the country with success, and turnips, cabbage and potatoes have long been adjuncts of hay raising. But the climate prevents most of the usual crops from flourishing. They lack hot summer sun for ripening and in some seasons even the potato crops may fail. Since 1930, when hothouses utilizing volcanic heat were built, tomatoes and green vegetables are grown in quantity. Grapes and bananas do well, though the latter are more a curiosity than a regular crop. The beautiful roses, orchids and other exotic cut flowers in

Reykjavik florist shops are products of volcanism. Pansies, corn flowers, tulips and other hardy flowers flourish outdoors in the moist cool climate, growing to enormous sizes and having intense colors. Gardens surrounding private homes, and the public parks, are bright splashes of color.

Like her Scandinavian cousins, Iceland relies heavily on cooperatives. About sixty-five per cent of the nation trades partly or wholly through cooperatives. The Federation of Icelandic Cooperative Societies was founded in 1902 and owns huge properties in all parts of the country. In addition to the usual export-import activities, they operate numerous factories.

There are few wild animals in Iceland and none of any economic importance. White fox were formerly numerous but have been deliberately exterminated in many districts as lamb

Beautiful gardens at Akureyri, Iceland.

killers. In 1771 reindeer were imported from Norway and placed in the interior. They increased and were killed for food until 1906 when the herd was in danger of being exterminated from overhunting. Since, they have been protected by law. Mink and other similar farms were started in Iceland some years ago. Some of the mink escaped and multiplied in their wild state until now they are considered a threat to salmon fishing and some of the island's bird life. Farmers usually kill them on sight because they raid the hen houses.

There are no reptiles in Iceland, no frogs and little insect life. In summer the only bothersome little creatures are the midges which are numerous in certain lake areas, like Myvatn in northern Iceland.

In summertime Iceland has numerous bird visitors. Because of the lack of trees they are easy to sight and identify. Only a few stay the year round, the most important being the ptarmigan which is hunted, eaten with relish, and even exported. Swans and the now rare sea eagle, falcons and eider ducks are on the roster. Icelanders use the down gathered from the nests of the eider ducks for bed covers, though they mostly sell it.

Iceland falcons, which resemble the Greenland variety but are slightly larger, were famous and highly prized throughout Europe during the Middle Ages for their brilliant hawking performances. They swiftly overtake their prey high in the air, stun the victim with a blow and catch it in their talons before it falls to earth. During the heyday of falconry, Icelandic falcons were a favorite gift or bribe from one king to another, because of their rarity and the difficulties involved in procuring them. When Iceland had a king, his escutcheon was a silver falcon on a blue ground. The bird has always been protected in Iceland, but stealing the young was one of the privileges permitted those of royal blood; otherwise, the punishment was severe.

The great auk, a bird that somewhat resembled the Antarctic penguin and is distantly related, used to abound in Iceland. They are now extinct, the last one having been killed in 1844. Gannet gulls occupy the rocky cliffs where the great auk used to nest, and charming little puffins still abound on the steep shores;

The rocky ledges of the cliffs of Grimsey are the nesting places for thousands of birds.

for instance, on the little island of Grimsey, just across the Arctic Circle from Iceland's northern coast.

In common with all the other Scandinavian countries, Iceland has a state church. It is Lutheran, and all her clergymen are civil servants. This does not mean that there is not complete freedom of religion in the country; there is. The Icelander prides himself on his liberality in matters of religion, as in other freedoms, and the tradition of the clergy from the year 1000, when Iceland embraced Christianity by an act of parliament, has always been liberal and flexible. But only about 1,000 Icelanders belong to denominations outside the Lutheran; many belong to no church at all.

In addition to the state religion, Iceland may be said to have a second religion which is a kind of nature worship. Most Ice-

Winter sports are popular now throughout Iceland.

landers seem to be passionately fond of their northern landscape and never cease to praise and admire it in painting and poetry, in song and story. There is scarcely a hill or farm or mountain that is not the subject of a poem, or has not been mentioned or described in one of the sagas. Here in Ultima Thule geography, history and literature are so tightly joined and braided as to be inseparable.

Many Icelanders are intensely interested in spiritualism and this includes the clergy. Whether or not there is a connection with the national interest in geneology which amounts to a mild kind of ancestor hero worship, is debatable. But their concern with spiritualism is one more facet of the complicated Icelandic character.

Only a hundred years ago Iceland was one of the poorest countries in the world. Her resources were few and the future looked so grim that about one in ten of her people left even the beloved island whose praises they had celebrated in song and saga for a thousand years. The high intellectual tradition nourished the spirit but not the body. The first of the migrants accompanied Brigham Young from Nauvoo, Illinois, on the master march and settled at Spanish Fork, Utah. Probably the next considerable settlement was on Washington Island in Lake Michigan. There followed colonies in Nova Scotia, Dakota Territory and Manitoba. During the last fifty years many Icelanders have moved from the United States to Canada and three-quarters of those now in North America, probably less than 50,000, are in the provinces of Manitoba, Saskatchewan and Alberta.

But today Iceland is prosperous. Her numbers have increased and they are among the healthiest people in the world. Her children are rosy-cheeked and sturdy. Now no one wants to leave Iceland except for pleasure trips, but some foreigners want to settle there—enough to produce restriction laws. Iceland is a member of the United Nations and of NATO. The construction of NATO defenses was formerly carried out by the United States, but in 1954 Icelandic contractors took over the expansion work at Keflavik airport. In 1956 there is a strong feeling that Iceland should take over the management of its own NATO station.

To sum up, then, Iceland is physically a sub-Arctic land of glaciers, volcanoes, lava deserts and waterfalls. She has survived earthquakes, volcanic eruptions, starvation and disease—not only to survive but actually to prosper under these trying conditions, largely through the personality and character of the people. They are brought up on a rich and satisfying diet of the heroic deeds of their ancestors from saga times. Icelanders learned early to bear misfortunes with calm dignity. They have turned handicap into asset and utilized every creative means to improve the lot of the country. Throughout the process of transforming a land of few resources into a flourishing democracy, they have been comforted and cheered by the noble words and deeds of their forefathers.

IV

Soviet Sector:

COLOSSUS IN THE ARCTIC

Soviet children leaving school in the afternoon.

ONE *Biggest, Coldest and Busiest*

THE Soviet sector of the Arctic is a land of immensities! It is the biggest, the coldest, the most densely populated of all the northern lands. It has the deepest permafrost ever recorded, the largest polar metropolis in the world, more weather and scientific stations, more icebreakers, more *activity*, than any of its neighbors circling the Pole.

Nearly half of the entire land area in the Arctic is Soviet soil. The Cold Pole of the world lies within its borders. Formerly thought to be Verkhoyansk, where a temperature of 93° below zero, Fahrenheit, has been recorded, the title is now held by Oimekon farther south—indeed, south of the Arctic Circle. Where other countries count their northernmost populations in thousands, the USSR can do it in millions. Two thousand feet of permanently frozen subsoil have been found at Nordvik in northern Siberia, a world record. Far and away the greatest polar metropolis in the world is the ice-free port of Murmansk where, in 1939, more than 117,000 people dwelt as far north as the northernmost coast of Alaska where our biggest town numbers less than 117 dozen.

In Alaska, Canada and Greenland together we have less than one million people who live farther north than Edmonton, North America's most northerly big city. The Soviet Union has more than 100 million who live farther north than that and with colder winters than ours.

A cross section of the daily life of the citizens of the Soviet North reveals extensive coal, oil and numerous other mineral developments as well as large- and small-scale agriculture. As in all underdeveloped countries where highways and railroads are few, or nonexistent, the airplane plays an important role in the transportation picture. The use of huge Siberian river systems, and in the last twenty-five or so years, the development of the Northern Sea Route, to the north of Asia, have all helped to provide a transportation system for this bustling land, whose actual size defies imagination.

To capture some inkling of the vastness of this area, start at the main port of the northern fishing fleet, Murmansk, just east of Finland. Travel steadily and you will have to cross 160 degrees of longitude and 4,000 miles of territory before reaching the easternmost Soviet point. Then you will be at Big Diomede Island in Bering Strait, from which it is only a three-mile walk in winter to Little Diomede Island, part of Alaska. You can see and shout from one hemisphere to another on a clear, cold day, from one day of the week to another. For between the rocky little islands runs the boundary between the Western and Eastern hemispheres and the International Date Line which separates one day of the week from the next. When it is Monday on Little Diomede, it is Tuesday on Big Diomede. But Bering Strait separates far more than geographical entities. It also divides symbolically two cultures, the Soviet and the Western, each with its own strikingly different political and historical concepts.

The Eskimos who live on the two Diomede Islands are related to one another; before World War II they visited freely across the strait, blissfully ignoring man-made boundaries and treaties. This informal handling of international relations stopped abruptly when wartime restrictions went into effect in Alaska and

ABOVE *The Russian island of Big Diomede, looking at it from the north and facing south.* BELOW *Dog sleds meet an airplane which has just returned from another sector of the Soviet Arctic.*

Siberia, and they have never been lifted. Now, in addition to geographical boundaries, a mist of fear and suspicion also divides the islands. No one leaves or enters Big Diomede without permission.

Within the USSR as a whole there are said to be 177 distinguishable nationalities speaking 125 different languages and dialects. In Siberia alone—that is, the Asiatic section of the Soviet North—there are said to be 28 million people. Of these, eighty per cent are Russians and the remainder are members of native groups that live mainly in the northern section.

As one moves eastward, the population becomes sparser, and so does the percentage of Russians. In the extreme northeast it is the native people who far outnumber the Russians. Eskimos and Eskimo-like peoples seem to us more colorful and in a way more interesting than the rest. Their names are strange and exotic—Chukchis, Koryaks, Yukaghirs, Chuvantzy, Eskimos, Ainus, Ostiaks, Lamuts, Nentsi and Lopars. They live by hunting, trapping, fishing, reindeer herding, or various combinations of the four. Some are nomads, following their game on foot or horse; others follow the reindeer herds across the prairies as they seek fresher pastures. Some live in villages and towns and vary their modes of life according to the seasons. Many are now educated city dwellers with only their special faces and romantic names left to distinguish them from their Russian neighbors.

A few groups like the Kurilians, Anauls and Omnoks, were entirely wiped out when the Russians moved eastward into Siberia. Large segments of other native groups were killed by gunfire, and even more by white man's disease, so that now some peoples, formerly numerous, number only a handful. The more isolated a community was, the better its chance to survive and increase. For 200 years the Siberian natives resisted the Russian drive into their territory with varying success, but eventually all were conquered. After the conquest they decreased steadily in numbers into the nineteenth century, when the last native uprisings took place—the Kamchadals in 1830, the Aleuts and Alaskan Eskimos in 1855, and the Samoyeds (now known as the Nentsi) in 1841.

Early in the 1930's the territory of these peoples was divided by the Soviet Government into National Districts. Among the sixteen most numerous groups an alphabet was introduced for the first time. In Leningrad the Institute of the Peoples of the North was founded to educate selected members of the various groups, who then returned home to pass on to their own people what they had learned. Private trading was "liquidated," in many cases cooperatives being substituted; but all activities, whether commercial or political, came under the direction of the Northern Sea Route Administration, in Leningrad.

Tundra composes something like the northern ten per cent of the Soviet Union. This is a Russian word meaning a low, marshy plain, generally unforested, which has long, cold winters with short days. Its summers are relatively brief and cool and the hours of daylight long. The extreme low winter temperatures, and the brevity of the summer, are responsible for the small amount of precipitation. So little, in fact, that many want to class this section with the desert regions of the world. Below the vegetation cover is permafrost, as there is in much of the Soviet Union—nearly half of the entire country, the experts say. The word tundra is sometimes applied to similar areas in North America, as well as Europe, although barren grounds and arctic prairie are commoner in North America.

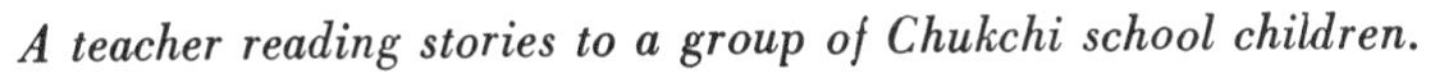

A teacher reading stories to a group of Chukchi school children.

The so-called arctic tundra, the northernmost section of the belt that stretches across the USSR, is not only treeless but virtually shrubless, too, except along river beds and in sheltered places. Vegetation is generally scant, but the flowering plants of the arctic tundra are famous for the abundance of their blossoms, their great size, and the brilliance of their colors.

What the Russians call the wooded tundra is a transition area between the treeless places to the north and the thick forests to the south. As the wooded tundra becomes more thickly forested, it eventually becomes *taiga,* which signifies a coniferous forest. Pine and fir trees dominate the western sections; toward the Urals they merge with Siberian larch, which extends farthest north of all the trees and covers more mountainous areas.

From the very heart of Asia three mighty river systems descend to cleave Siberia from south to north. The Yenisei-Selenga, the Ob-Irtysh, and the Lena, fifth, sixth and eighth longest river systems in the world, all flow north toward the Polar Sea. Their tributaries reach in every direction, almost touching the farthest branches of neighbor streams. Small rivers join the larger ones to make a webbed pattern across the Soviet North. The predominant slope of the northern continents, North American as well as Eurasian, is toward the north, a condition which encourages the formation of long river systems.

This giant network of rivers was the first, and for centuries the only means of transportation for Russian Asia. Liquid in summer, it was far more hospitable to boats and small ships than the more northerly Polar Sea. During the long winters the rivers, large and small, were frozen glassy, hard as concrete boulevards to foot or sledge. Mainly the sledges were drawn by horses or reindeer, but also by dogs. These were the paths by which Russians explored the unknown, roadless land with comparative safety, permitting them to extend their trade farther and farther eastward till Alaska, the New World, loomed on the horizon. Siberian rivers still retain their importance in the economic and transportation picture of the Soviet Union, but now they are helped by the Northern Sea Route, the yearly, regular use of the Northeast Passage.

TWO Early Trade: Mammoth Ivory and Furs

FROM Marco Polo's thirteenth century onward, Europe dreamed of finding a sea route to the Indies, to replace the long, hazardous overland journey across Asia. The search reached its greatest flowering during Queen Elizabeth's reign, when the hope of finding a Northwest Passage to China gripped men's minds and spurred them to undertake new and dangerous voyages.

But the Northwest Passage failed to materialize. Northwestern Europe then turned her eyes in the opposite direction to weigh the chances of a North*east* Passage around Asia. The Company of Merchant Adventurers was formed and the first English expedition to the Indies, via the East, set sail, commanded by Captain-General Sir Hugh Willoughby. Of his three ships only Richard Chancellor's penetrated as far as the White Sea at the present site of Archangel. Local fishermen told Chancellor the country was called Russia, or Muscovy, and was ruled by a great Tsar, Ivan Vasilievich, known to us as Ivan the Terrible.

Chancellor and his men were invited to visit the court at Moscow. They made a fifteen hundred mile overland journey to accept the invitation. Amidst breath-taking splendor, they were received cordially by Ivan, and delivered to him the letters they carried from their own sovereign. The trading rights they sought were granted, and two years later the name of the Merchant Adventurers was changed to the Muscovy Company. A flourishing trade, chiefly in furs and mammoth ivory, was established between the two countries. Chancellor wrote an account of his experiences, and for the first time Englishmen were privileged to read their own eyewitness accounts of the geography, people, religion, court and manners of the Russian Empire.

The lucrative mammoth ivory trade which grew up as a result of Chancellor's voyage was new to England; but this ivory trade with China, formerly thought by us to have started in medieval times, has now been traced as far back as 500 B.C. Perhaps before the Chinese, the Greeks and the Romans knew its source, they were handling mammoth ivory, transporting it from trading center to trading center over thousands of miles.

Just what is a mammoth? He is the most recent of several forms of prehistoric elephant. He roamed the earth in Pleistocene times, and the last of his breed was killed perhaps more

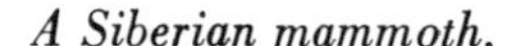

A Siberian mammoth.

than ten thousand years ago. Stone Age man knew him well. He drew and painted his portrait on European cave walls with accuracy and beauty. He discovered that mammoth ivory tusks made better implements of a certain kind than bone, and that his flesh was delicious to eat.

The northern, or woolly, mammoth ranged in a circumpolar belt through northern Europe and Siberia, Alaska, northern Canada and a northerly strip of the United States, always north of 40° North latitude. Equipped by nature to cope with cold, he followed the retreating glaciers northward many ages ago. His cousins, the Jeffersonian and imperial mammoths, even larger in size, roamed in more southerly areas, but the woolly mammoth preferred the northerly grassy tundra. The Siberian mammoth was about twelve feet tall at the shoulder, and had a long thick coat of coarse black hair, sometimes twenty inches in length, which hung round him like a robe, reminding one of a muskox. Beneath it was a shorter, soft, brownish-red wool lying close to the skin, adding to his bulky look. His ears were smaller than those of an Indian elephant, about twelve inches long, and he had a short tail that narrowed gradually, ending like an elephant's with a brush of long, stiff bristles. Beside his warm fur coat he had additional protection against the cold in a layer of fat about three and a half inches thick which encased his body. But by far the most striking single feature of the woolly mammoth was, and is, his tusk. Two huge, curling ivory prongs that could measure nine or ten feet in length, weighed an average—for large males—288 pounds each. Compare these with the modern African elephant whose tusks weigh a mere forty or fifty pounds.

If the last member of his family perished so long ago, how dare we describe the mammoth so accurately, telling with confidence his height, and width, and the color of his hair, and the length of his tail, even his fatness? How is it that we know the names of those plants which made up his vegetarian diet? These are details that could not be furnished by a cave painting, however artistic. Permafrost is the answer. Thanks to its deep-freeze qualities, entire mammoths have been found preserved, with their meat still fresh, their hair intact, and even one with grass still in his mouth. Undigested stomach contents have provided us with his menu, and these plants were the same that are still found to this day in northern Siberia. Grasses and sedges were his mainstay, and in winter he fed on arctic willow and other northerly dwarf plants. Wild animals, domestic dogs, primitive and modern man alike, have eaten the flesh of these shaggy mammoths, thriving on beasts that lived thousands of years ago, some say hundreds of thousands. Fossil ice and frozen mud, unthawed for millenniums, shut out both air and heat to be the natural freezer lockers which preserved for us knowledge of this animal, the first extinct beast discovered by man.

The tips of a mammoth's tusks were sharpened and used effectively for combat purposes. It must have been an awesome sight for ancient Stone Age man to come upon this mountain of a beast, his long, white, gleaming tusks contrasting sharply against his dark, shaggy coat. In old age the ivory tusks would begin to curve inward, sometimes until they actually crossed each other, making them useless as a defensive weapon.

Primitive man, with no tools capable of subduing this giant, invented ingenious methods for his capture. Excavators have found huge earthen pits into which he lured the mammoth, and once trapped, killed him by hurling large stones at him.

A famous Dutch traveler who was ambassador to China, Ysbrants Ides, is said to be the earliest to report the discovery of a frozen mammoth in Siberia. That was in 1692. He also told that the Ostiaks, Yakuts and Tungus peoples he encountered, like the Eskimos of Alaska and Canada, believed the mammoth to be a living creature who dwelt underground. They felt certain that if he emerged above the earth he would die, and pointed to the evidence for this belief—all the mammoths they had ever seen were dead. It was supposed that mammoths died instantly when they breathed the warm air above ground. Since Ides' time, frozen mammoths have been discovered often, and in great numbers. Estimates range from 20,000 to 50,000 found during the last 200 years.

ABOVE *An illustration from Ysbrants Ides' narrative of his journey into Siberia, showing the winter clothing of a Tungus native.* BELOW *A drawing by a Dutch artist showing Russians traveling by dog sled in Siberia.*

The color of fossil ivory can vary from pure white that looks so fresh one might think the animal newly killed, to the color of stained mahogany. Bright blue tusks, walnut, russet, and brick-red colored tusks have also been found, although the most brilliant of these are surface colorings which do not penetrate throughout. The commonest mammoth ivory is a creamy color, often streaked with brown and grey.

Europe's fossil ivory trade flourished for a relatively short time following Chancellor's voyage. Ice that blocked and sometimes crushed the trading vessels, fog that confused and delayed, finally resulted in a series of disasters. English merchants were so discouraged by the loss of lives and profits that they turned their backs on the Northeast Passage and concentrated once more on finding a Northwest Passage.

But if the English gave up, not so the Russian traders who were just discovering the riches of Siberia, or Sibir, as it was called then. No need for them to make long sea voyages when just beyond the borders of their own country lived primitive Samoyed and other Eskimo-like natives who delighted in bringing them sable and fox skins to exchange for bits of iron and the cheapest of trade goods. Small scale commercial trading began, with each Russian merchant eager to keep as a "trade secret" news of the fabulous return for a modest investment. Good news is difficult to suppress, however; despite all effort, word of the fur "gold mine" seeped out, eventually reaching official circles. For the first time royal interest was awakened.

Why should the Imperial Government be interested in the fur trade? Because the chief trader in what grew to be a vast fur empire, then as now, *was* the government.

A tribute called *yassak,* a tax paid in furs, was collected from the Tungus, Samoyeds and Ostiaks, and a ten per cent tax payable in the choicest furs was collected from all Russian traders and trappers. Everyone helped to support the Tsar in the gorgeous manner to which he was accustomed. In addition the government, or the Tsar (in those days of absolute monarchs the terms were interchangeable), retained for itself the right to buy the finest pelts from merchant and hunter alike. His Imperial Highness held the monopoly on all sable and black fox skins sold to China, and thereby developed a highly profitable foreign trade. Russian furs found their way to German as well as Chinese fur markets and were the most important single item in all sixteenth century Russian commerce, both foreign and domestic. Most of the fur that produced this wealth for the government came from Siberia. With every tenth skin caught by a native or sold by a merchant automatically becoming his, it is easy to see why the Tsar took more than a casual interest in the eastward expansion of the fur industry.

The traders who went after the skins had to leave familiar lands behind and enter darkly unknown places, there to deal with unpredictable and possibly murderous strangers whose language they could not speak. Their motive grows all the clearer when we learn that at this time a pair of black fox skins would bring their owner one hundred and ten rubles. With that sum he could buy fifty-five acres of land, build a good cabin, acquire five horses, twenty head of cattle, twenty sheep, several dozen

A fur warehouse where fox and bear pelts are being aired and processed.

fowl, and still have half of his capital left. A single successful trading expedition could make him rich for life.

The famous Strogonov family, the most powerful capitalists of their day, held a monopoly for trading in northeastern Russia, and eventually controlled all the natural wealth of the Siberian north. They owned salt and iron mines, but by far the greatest source of their wealth was the fur trade. Ivan the Terrible himself commissioned the Strogonovs to buy sables for him, especially "prime sables." These were the most superb pelts of all which the Russians called "odinets," meaning unequalled. They were taken at just the right season of the year when their fur was thickest and glossiest and the color most beautiful. They were never handled like ordinary skins which were packed and sold in bales, but were cared for individually and brought the highest prices.

Toward the end of the sixteenth century the Strogonovs found their peace and prosperity threatened by bands of Cossacks. These were men who had fled their native lands as serfdom settled heavily over the Russian peasant. The Cossacks organized themselves into republics of free men; and, recognizing neither class nor private property distinctions, developed into disciplined professional soldiers who conquered and plundered at will.

With tact and diplomatic skill, Maxim Strogonov offered the Cossack leader, Yermak Timofeyev, every material assistance if he and his men would conquer Siberia, the wild and untamed land to the east. Yermak rose to the bait and in 1581 emerged on the first of his series of successful military expeditions. Thus in one move the Strogonovs were rid of an explosive, troublemaking force and the Cossack's newly acquired taste for war and adventure was satisfied.

Year by year, generation by generation, the Cossacks penetrated farther eastward. En route their children were born, matured, married and produced children to replenish the ranks and carry on the conquest. Settlers, hunters and traders followed in the Cossack wake until, more than a hundred years later, they had reached the eastern shore of the Asiastic continent, where

Kamchatka Peninsula hooks its long claw into the Pacific Ocean.

History books were nearly unanimous in repeating the legend that Siberia was "discovered" by the Strogonovs and "conquered" by Yermak. But a few scholars point out that the citizens of the republic of Novgorod, which first ruled the Russian North, had been reaching the Ob River for two centuries before Yermak made his first foray.

THREE

“*Sable-rich*” *Mangazeya*

NOT long ago a marriage between history and archaeology produced evidence that in 1600 and earlier, the communication between Russia and Siberia was far more extensive than any one had previously imagined. Historians examining the archives of various remote Siberian towns encountered repeated references to Mangazeya, a town they had always thought of as mythical. Archaeologists were sent out to find the dead city, and in a sense to bring it back to life. For to an archaeologist the pieces of pottery, the dated coins, the broken bits of glass and earthenware —whatever emerges when they excavate a site—tells a factual story of the people who dwelt there. Even what they do *not* find can be most informative.

Buried weapons, or their absence, will tell the temper of a people. Imported articles tell a social history—whom they were in touch with, and when. Kitchen middens, the archaeologist's polite word for garbage heap, tells what was eaten, how it was prepared and how it was secured, whether by hunting or agriculture. Were they prosperous, healthy, artistic? The archaeologist knows the answers to these questions and to many more.

Mangazeya, a town which we now know to have flourished

during the first half of the sixteen hundreds on the eastern bank of the Taz River, is a good example of a "resurrected" community. Thanks to such normally dreary sources as tax lists, Imperial decrees and official correspondence, its site was discovered in 1900, but not until extensive diggings were made in 1946 was a connected story revealed.

Mangazeya started out as a meeting place for trappers and merchants, and was so successful that it soon claimed the attention of the government. Tsar Boris Godunov in 1600 sent an expedition to conquer it. But the natives, as well as the local Russians, knew they would be heavily taxed if they surrendered to the Tsar's men; so they resisted, at first successfully, but the following year they were conquered. A new town arose on the site of the old trading post. It contained a typical wooden fortress, complete with governor and all the trappings that accompany Imperial rule.

Mangazeya continued to flourish; but now yassak, or tribute, was imposed, and the finest sables reserved for the Tsar. So many sables of first quality passed through Mangazeya that it was called "sable-rich" Mangazeya. From the Imperial bookkeepers we know that between sixty and a hundred thousand sable skins passed through the little town *every year.* Recalling the wealth represented by a single skin, we find here a worthy competitor to the riches of the Indies. A trading fair was held every year in the town, swelling its normal population of a few hundred to over a thousand.

Within the fortified log wall enclosure, with its five watch towers, were two churches, some inns for visitors, a customs house, a market place with twenty shops, warehouses for grain, salt and gunpowder, two public houses, a bath house and a prison. The Cossack garrison was augmented by a company of musketeers with cannons.

Normally it wouldn't seem strange to have a thousand people assemble in a remote Siberian town for a trading fair. But when one remembers how far from civilized places men had to travel to reach Mangazeya, by what primitive means, through what perilous and virtually unknown arctic seas, then it becomes doubly remarkable. They had to navigate the "Icy Sea" almost a third of the distance through the present Northern Sea Route, to reach Mangazeya. Voyages were made in *kochi,* flat-bottomed boats, of six to seven tons, which were both seaworthy and transportable across short portages. Their flat bottoms permitted them to enter shallow waters where vessels of deeper draught dared not venture.

The route led from the White Sea through Yugorski Shar, across Yamal Peninsula by river and portage, through the Gulf of Ob, across it into Taz Bay at the mouth of the Taz River, then upstream to the townsite. This "great ocean sea" route was preferred to the lengthier and costlier southern overland routes. Larger cargoes could be transported and the trip from Archangel completed in four and a half weeks, compared to two and a half months required for the overland journey. In 1936 this same route was re-examined and found so excellent that, more than 300 years after its discovery, it was put into use again without change.

But at the height of Mangazeya's prosperity new trouble was brewing. Following Chancellor, both Englishmen and Hollanders began trading in Muscovy. They heard of Mangazeya and tried unsuccessfully to reach it. The Russian merchants were by no means blind to the foreign interest in their miracle city. As strange ships approached closer and closer on successive tries, the government also grew fearful that they might succeed in reaching it and in finding ways to avoid customs duties and taxes. A military expedition from Western Europe could conceivably attack and capture the town. Officials decided that foreigners should be forbidden to use the seaway. First a government decree in 1619 forbade navigation between the White and Barents seas, so the last leg of the route had to be made overland. In 1667 all navigation by kochi was forbidden, and the entire trip had to be made overland. Despite protests the decree was enforced and Russian exploration of the Northeast Passage, so auspiciously begun, was cut off for fear that foreigners might share in the spoils. When Mangazeya's life as a seaport ended, its decay as a fur trading center began.

FOUR

Two Continents or One?

IN 1655 a Cossack named Semen Ivanovich Dezhnev, handed a clerk at Yakutsk, Siberia, the report of a journey he had made seven years before. It told how, setting out in an open boat on a fur hunting expedition, he had traveled farther and farther eastward from the Kolyma River until he reached the very end of the continent. He had rounded Chukotsk Peninsula, passing the northeasternmost point of Asia, and been driven out to sea. By great good fortune he had managed to land south of the Anadyr River. He had then traveled overland 1,500 miles to hand in his report at the proper administrative center, for he had made a momentous discovery. Asia and North America were two separate continents, not one, as many believed.

We don't know whether the clerk who accepted the report even read it. But instead of sending it on to his superiors he placed it in a routine file, and the news for which not only his own nation, but the entire world was eager, went no farther.

A generation later Dezhnev's strait was "discovered" by and named for Vitus Bering. Another two centuries passed before the Cossack's report was uncovered and the northeastern corner of Asia renamed for its rightful discoverer, Cape Dezhnev.

During the years the report was gathering dust in Yakutsk, emperors dispatched expeditions, sea captains forced new paths through ice-packed waters, and explorers traveled overland for thousands of miles. Men and ships alike were sacrificed in attempting to solve the riddle to which Dezhnev had earlier found the answer.

Peter the Great, who founded Russia's Academy of Sciences, was from childhood and throughout his turbulent life fascinated by boats and sea voyages. He had many plans for increasing the scientific knowledge of his country, among these the series of explorations which came to be known as the Great Northern Expedition. With justice this has been called "one of the most remarkable undertakings in the history of science."

In 1724, Peter had sent Bering, a Dane in Russian service, on his first expedition, to determine whether America and Asia were joined. Bering returned in 1730 with few practical results beyond "discovering" Bering Strait. The burning question was still unanswered. The Great Northern Expedition to this region, starting in 1733, was again commanded by Bering, and lasted for a decade. It was not one but several expeditions, involved many hundreds of men and cost millions of rubles.

We know why Dezhnev's discovery was unknown in St. Petersburg, but more difficult to fathom is why the Northern Expedition was dispatched despite a remarkable book written by Philip Johann von Strahlenberg. Strahlenberg was a Swedish nobleman, officer of King Charles the XII. He fought valorously in the battle of Poltava against the Russians, but was captured, and with many others, exiled to Siberia. For the thirteen years of his exile he used his time to gather information of every sort about Siberia. In 1723 he returned to Sweden and seven years later published a book which clearly shows the separation of Asia and America, marking in great detail the coastline, rivers, towns and even the names of the numerous Siberian tribes and which lands each occupied. Peter the Great knew all about Strahlenberg; he had even offered him a job as he passed through the capital on his way home to Sweden. The exile had declined, but Peter kept a copy of his wonderful map. The mystery of why it was ignored and Bering sent to do it all again has never been solved.

By the time Bering finally saw the North American continent in southeastern Alaska, he was sixty years old and thoroughly worn out. After fifteen years of hard struggle he seemed to his men, many of whom had already died of scurvy, to be willing to die. But gloom and pessimism are symptoms of scurvy and Bering was doubtless affected, too, by the deficiency disease. On the island which bears his name and lies appropriately between the two continents, the Dane who had labored so many years for the Russians died in December, 1741.

Gold was discovered in Siberia. By the middle of the nineteenth century production of the precious metal reached its peak, excepting most recent times. As gold mining became an important industry, agriculture grew with it, to supply food for the workers. Political exiles and newly arrived settlers provided cheap labor to work the farms, and before long Siberia was pro-

A group of exiles crossing the Yenisei River in Siberia.

ducing more food than she could use. When the emancipation of the serfs in 1861 freed huge numbers of peasants, many flocked to Western Siberia, more than doubling its population by the end of the century when it reached five million. Western Siberia, between the Ural Mountains and the Yenisei River, is almost entirely a level plain sloping gradually to the arctic shore, and proved ideal for farming.

As a result of over exploitation, gold mining began to decline after 1847. An abundance of capital and few investment opportunities encouraged Moscow merchants to buy up huge estates and turn them into farming "factories." Peasant cooperatives came into being, too, producing and exporting butter on a large scale. Siberian farmers became wealthy. A good yardstick for measuring the well-being of a farmer is the number of horses he owns. In central Russia between thirty-three and forty per cent of the farms had no horses, and manpower alone accounted for the heavy tasks of ploughing, cultivating and reaping. But only ten per cent of Siberia's farms lacked horses in 1912. This wealth enabled Siberian peasants to buy more farming machinery than those in Russia and thereby produce more crops per acre.

Visitors to Siberia noticed other differences. Physically the Siberians seemed healthier and hardier, and most striking was their high spirit. They were rugged, independent and had a vital quality lacking in their European brothers. Siberia had never known serfdom and perhaps this produced a freedom of spirit. Here was found "no melancholy, no religion of suffering," frequently associated with the Russian peasant.

In the late nineteenth century, as Siberian farmers looked about for foreign markets accessible to the sea where they might sell their excess produce, interest in the Northeast Passage was revived. They wanted to ship north, downstream along their rivers, and then east and west along the north coast of Asia to the markets of the Atlantic and Pacific. As consumers, Siberians also hoped the development of a sea route would bring down the high prices they were compelled to pay for manufactured goods.

ABOVE *Different varieties of grain being inspected at a state selection station.*
BELOW *Siberian frost-resistant creeping apple trees. A shallow layer of snow will protect them against freezing.*

Norwegians, Englishmen, Danes and Swedes, as well as Russians, played roles in the pageant of finding and developing a commercial water route to connect Siberia with the outside world. Norwegian sealers entering the Kara Sea discovered rich sealing grounds to which they returned year after year, hoping to keep the knowledge a secret from their competitors. An English sea captain, Joseph Wiggins, made many pioneering voyages over a twenty-year period, becoming a successful ice navigator and merchant in the process. The distinguished Swedish-Finnish scientist, Nils Adolph Erik Nordenskiöld, in 1875, started on the first complete and successful navigation of the Northeast Passage, finishing it the next year. While his motives were scientific rather than commercial, he and his backers knew that if science succeeded, commerce would too.

Mikhail Sidorov, owner of gold mines in the Yenisei River district, was primarily interested in finding a seaway to transport heavy machinery to his mines, but he eventually became more interested in helping the over-all development of the entire north country. He was the first to appreciate the significance of the great rivers Ob and Yenisei as a connecting link between central Siberia and the outside world. Sidorov backed his faith by offering a prize of 14,000 rubles for the first man to sail from the west to the Yenisei. He wrote articles, arranged international exhibits displaying the huge natural wealth of the North, in short devoted himself to his ideal. But he seemed alone in his enthusiasm. No one claimed his prize.

Another gold mining tycoon, Aleksandr Mikhailovich Sibiryakov, used his wealth to help finance men like Captain Wiggins and Nordenskiöld. For several years following the latter's historic voyage, there was some activity along the passage but it still remained virtually unused.

It was the building of the longest railroad in the world in 1893, the Trans-Siberian, which finally roused the government's interest in the Northeast Passage. If rails could be shipped in by boat to various points along the way and work could proceed simultaneously in several directions, the saving in time and money would be enormous. Moving first north to the Arctic Sea and then east along the north coast of the Old World, 1,600 tons of rails were shipped in by sea and then up-river, under the experienced supervision of Captain Wiggins.

Now it became apparent that though the route had been "discovered" it had never been properly explored and charted. Detailed hydrographic information was needed to insure its continued success. For a period of eleven years the government sponsored a series of scientific exploring expeditions, and in 1897, a historic date, the first icebreaker built for northern use was finished and named *Yermak* after the Cossack conqueror.

During the Russo-Japanese War every soldier and piece of equipment used against the Japanese had to be transported thousands of miles across Siberia on the Trans-Siberian Railroad, which had been completed in 1905. Soon it was badly overloaded, and the shipment of all non-military goods for Siberian farms and cities was stopped. Siberians began to go hungry, and then real famine broke out. The Northern Sea Route was

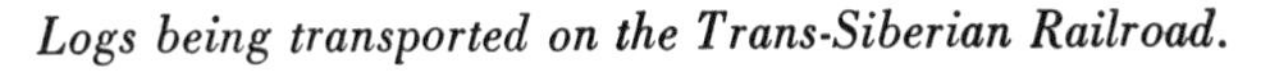
Logs being transported on the Trans-Siberian Railroad.

remembered, and became a genuine "life saver" when tons of desperately needed foodstuffs were shipped in by sea and river.

When the Russians lost the Russo-Japanese War, to many the key to the defeat lay in the transportation problem. The Trans-Siberian, despite its cost and boasted modernity, proved inadequate to serve the desperate needs of war. Some felt that disaster might have been exchanged for victory if the Russians had had a second string to their transportation bow, a really usable sea lane round the north of Siberia. Defense strategy at last proved the most effective spur to government action on a large scale.

Permanent telegraph and meteorological stations were now set up along the Arctic Sea Route to collect and relay weather and ice information. More icebreakers were constructed to keep shipping lanes and harbors open for longer periods and to free vessels caught in the ice. Commercial voyages were officially en-

Meteorological observations being taken in the Soviet Sector of the Arctic.

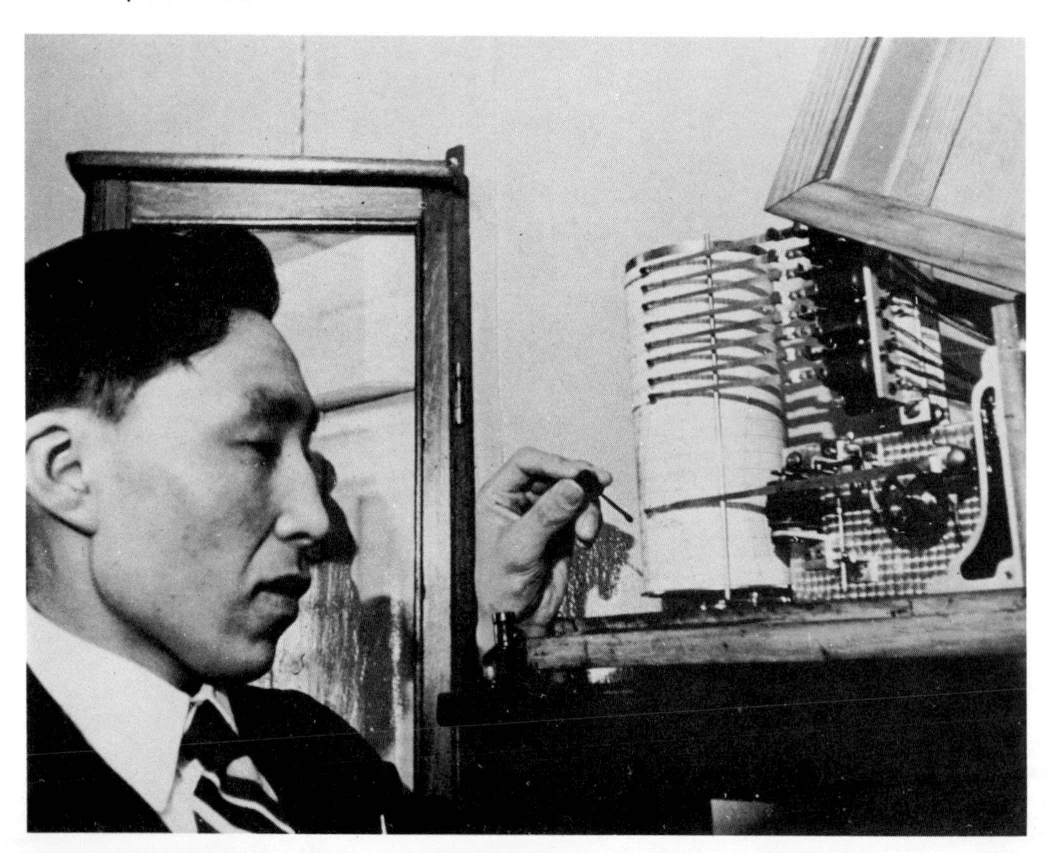

couraged. By the time of the 1917 Russian Revolution the sea route was a going concern, practical and successful.

The loud huzzahs of Soviet scientists for their own achievements back in the 1930's, the enthusiasm which led them to "discover" what was often well known in non-Russian circles, and to soft-pedal all pre-Soviet and non-Soviet activities, led many to think of the successful Northern Sea Route as a Soviet invention. True, the Soviets made the expansion and exploitation of the route a matter of policy, incorporating it into their Five Year Plans. It is also true that where the Imperial Government had been reluctant and parsimonious, the Soviets spent huge sums, and made belief in the success of the route a segment of the "party line." It was required that one be optimistic and enthusiastic about the expansion and development of the Soviet Arctic generally and the Sea Route particularly.

Every means was used by the government to excite and sustain interest in the northern program. Each new polar station that was built was played up in the newspapers and magazines. Any new geographical or scientific discovery made in the North was glorified immediately and lavishly in the press and on the radio. Polar explorers became the greatest heroes of the day, decorated, idolized and lionized. News of failure or unfavorable conditions was soft-pedaled except as it might add spice to a success story. Higher wages were offered for arctic posts, and the men who took them were acclaimed as "glorious polar heroes." Far more volunteered than could be used.

In trying to evaluate fairly the Soviet success or failure in the Arctic, it is well to remember the hard facts of geography—the Soviet population of ten millions north of the Arctic Circle, the many brand-new and other greatly expanded cities which have grown up to develop a local natural resource. We must credit them with the invention of a system of ice forecasting which works like our weather forecasting and enables their ships to get through ice-filled waters. They excel through long experience in the art of using icebreakers which has enabled them to extend the summer navigation to a maximum of four months under ideal weather conditions. They have expanded a handful of polar stations until they number more than one hundred along the northern coast and islands, and these supply regular information both to shipping and aviation. Probably the Soviet Union's most formidable superiority over North Americans is in their large supply of arctic-trained personnel. Men whose names first appeared in Russian arctic periodicals thirty years ago, still appear. They are still active in their various fields and are probably training youngsters as they work. We have a tendency to dodge into the North and out again. At most, a man works five or ten years in the North and then settles down to teaching or museum work. Not so the Soviets.

From our point of view the Northern Sea Route may not be what we would call an "economical success"; that is, for the

A view of the North Pole-4 drifting scientific station.

money and energy expended, profits are small. But we must remember that this is of little or no importance to the Soviets. They count the success or failure of such an enterprise from a different perspective. The advantages it gives them from a military and strategic point of view are great. It gives them an alternate to the Trans-Siberian Railroad, although not a year-round one. It is relatively invulnerable to attack from foreign ships. Important among their profits is the prestige they have gained among the native peoples living in the areas served by the route. These peoples are eager to please.

We know that Lend-Lease materials from the United States were shipped during World War II from the Bering Sea to the Soviet Union by the Northern Sea Route, some 452,000 tons of it. We know also from Russian acknowledgments that it all arrived. But the ships were manned by Russian sailors, so we have few details. We can speculate with a certain degree of accuracy on the many remarkable voyages that must have been made during this period, particularly by the Liberty ships, for they were bigger than any freighters used up to that time in the northern Soviet waters. A significant clue to the high value the Soviets must place on the route is the secrecy they maintain about it. Not much real information has come through since 1939!

It now seems certain that the Soviet Union is determined to make her frozen earth yield up its riches. Arctic oil is one reason she can claim half the reserves in the world. Her nickel reserves are second largest in the world and arctic Norilsk is an important reason why. Coal from Vorkhuta, gold from the Lena River, tin from Yakutsk, salt from Nordvik, all these are arctic places contributing a good share to the mineral wealth of their country. At each site processing plants have been built on the spot, instead of sending the materials long distances to manufacturing and refining centers, as we usually do.

During World War II the forty-mile railroad built in 1939 from coal-producing Vorkhuta to the nearest navigable river, was extended over the permafrost until it measured 1,000 miles and joined the main Soviet rail network. The coal thus made available replaced the supplies of Spitsbergen coal which the Soviets had relied on, which was cut off by the Germans. Limited production of Vorkhuta coal started in 1931, but again we have pathetically few bits of authentic information to complete the picture. Few reliable statistics about any strategic materials or activities have found their way to this country, although a careful reader of all Russian newspapers and periodicals by detective-story methods can extract some facts and speculate a good deal on others. We have some limited first-hand reports from prisoners of war which give us many hints but relatively few exact facts and figures. Further information comes to us from a new kind of prisoner, new at least to this country, the slave labor camp prisoner.

A large percentage of the road building, and virtually all the railroad construction and arctic mining in the Soviet Union, is accomplished through the use of slave labor. The number of such laborers in the country is estimated at the appalling number of from ten to fifteen millions. In the Kolyma district of northeastern Siberia alone it is thought that between one and a half and two million such workers are developing the rapidly expanding gold mining operations there.

Aside from the neatly dovetailing reports given us by escapees from these camps, and from some who have been released, the most devastating evidence of their existence and methods are found in the Soviet government's own documents which were brought to the attention of the world in 1952. From June to November in that year the United Nations investigated the slave labor situation throughout the world and the Soviet role in this was revealed.

Horrible as is the thought to us of using such a plan to build installations and maintain huge mines in the Soviet Union, we must not blind ourselves to the existence of the installations. Rather they should stand as a mighty challenge to the United States, Canada and Scandinavia to match, or better still, to excel, by *democratic* means, the utilization and development of the resources of *our* side of the polar world.

Acknowledgments

GRATEFUL ACKNOWLEDGMENT IS MADE FOR PERMISSION TO USE
THE FOLLOWING:

Photograph on page 126 from the *American Museum of Natural History*
Photograph on page 12 from *Associated Screen News Limited,* Canada
Photographs on pages 31, 35 from *Cliché Expéditions Polaires Françaises*
Photograph on page 107b from *Arni Eylands*
Photograph on page 45 from *Jacob Gayer,* courtesy of
the *National Geographic Society*
Photographs on pages 17, 19a, 21 from *Richard Harrington*
Photograph on page 77 from *C. J. Hubbard*
Photographs on pages 84a, 108, 114 from the *Iceland Tourist Bureau*
Photograph on page 121a from *Fred Machetanz*
Photographs on pages 80, 99, 109 from *Olafur K. Magnusson*
Photographs on pages 62, 139 from the *New York Public Library*
Photographs on pages 5, 10 from *Pan American World Airways*
Photographs on pages 51b, 67 from the *Royal Danish Ministry for Foreign Affairs*
Photographs on page 2 from the *Scandinavian Airlines*
Photographs on pages 61, 105b, 111, 113 from *Vigfus Sigurgeirsson*
Photographs on pages 118, 121b, 123, 131, 141, 143, 144, 146
from *Sovfoto*
Photographs on pages 129a, 129b from the *Stefansson Collection,*
Baker Library, Dartmouth College
Photograph on page 105a from the *United States Army Signal Corps*
Photographs on pages 51a, 65 from the *United States State Department*

Index

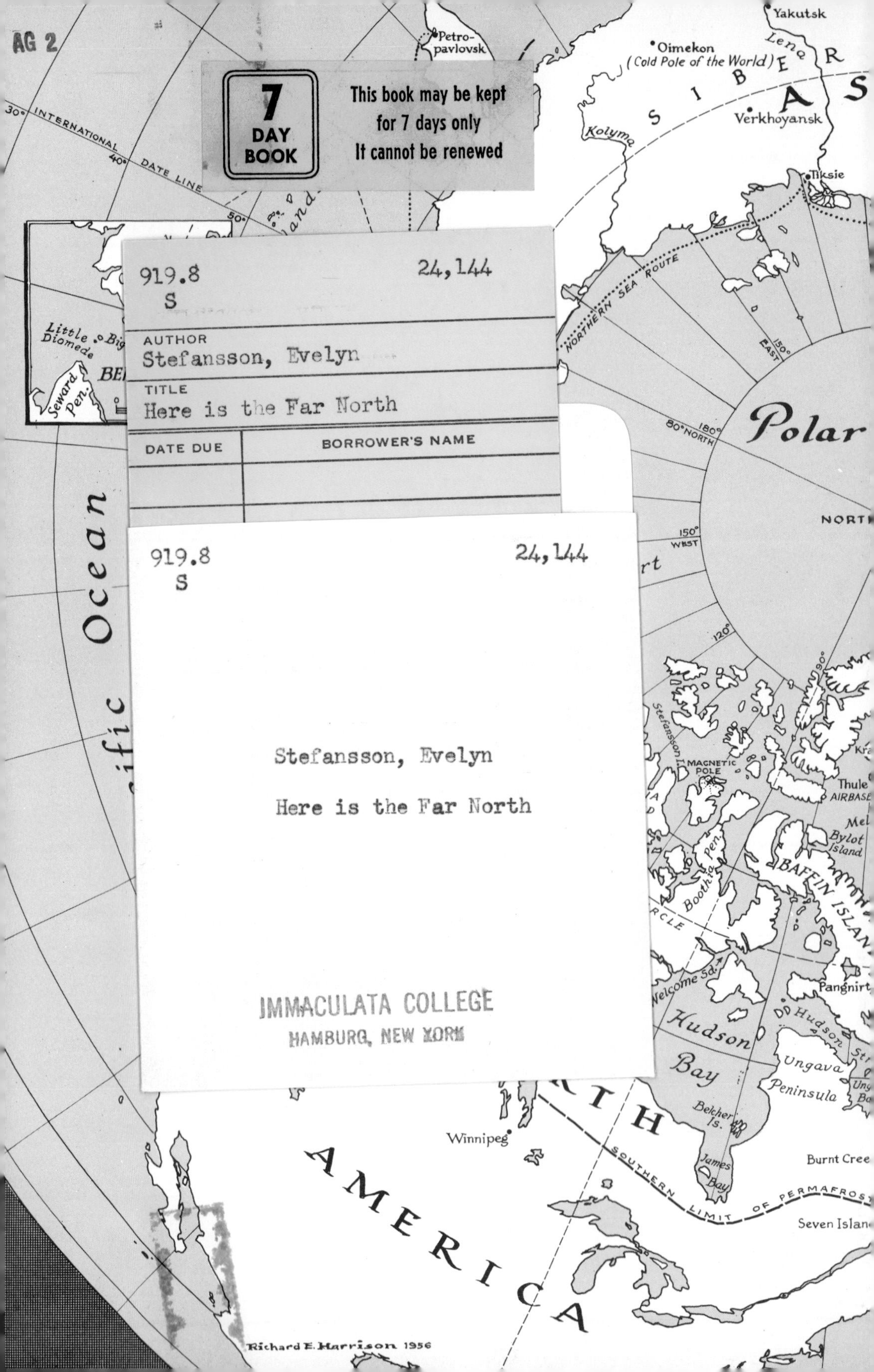
AG 2
7 DAY BOOK
This book may be kept
for 7 days only
It cannot be renewed
919.8
S
24,144
AUTHOR
Stefansson, Evelyn
TITLE
Here is the Far North
DATE DUE
BORROWER'S NAME
919.8
S
24,144
Stefansson, Evelyn
Here is the Far North
IMMACULATA COLLEGE
HAMBURG, NEW YORK
Yakutsk
Oimekon
(Cold Pole of the World)
Lena
SIBERIA
Verkhoyansk
Kolyma
Tiksie
Petro-
pavlovsk
INTERNATIONAL DATE LINE
NORTHERN SEA ROUTE
Little Diomede
Seward Pen.
Polar
80° NORTH
180°
150° EAST
150° WEST
120°
Ocean
Stefansson I.
MAGNETIC POLE
Thule AIRBASE
Bylot Island
BAFFIN ISLAND
Boothia Pen.
Welcome Sd.
Pangnirtung
Hudson Bay
Hudson Str.
Ungava Peninsula
Belcher Is.
James Bay
Winnipeg
AMERICA
SOUTHERN LIMIT OF PERMAFROST
Burnt Creek
Seven Islands
Richard E. Harrison 1956